Safe Practice in Physical Education

Safe Practice in

Physical Education

THE BRITISH ASSOCIATION OF ADVISERS AND LECTURERS IN PHYSICAL EDUCATION

Safe Practice in Physical Education

Copyright © The British Association of Advisers and Lecturers in Physical Education 1985, 1990

ISBN 1 871228 06 9

Original edition published 1979;
this revised edition published 1990 by
The British Association of Advisers and Lecturers in Physical Education

Design: Douglas Martin
Cover design: IT Design Associates
Illustrations: Michael Long

Produced and distributed on behalf of BAALPE by **White Line Press**,
60 Bradford Road, Stanningley, Leeds
LS28 6EF

All orders to be sent to White Line Press

Printed in Great Britain at the Alden Press, Oxford

Photographic credits

Cover photographs, clockwise from top:
Noel Whittall, Supersport, Noel Whittall, Supersport, Stephen Line

Contents

Acknowledgements	8
Abbreviations Used in the Text	8
Introduction	**9**

Part One	**PE, the Law and Safe Practice**	**11**
	Qualifications for Teaching PE	11
	General	*11*
	Primary schools	*11*
	Secondary schools	*12*
	Help from parents and other teachers	*13*
	PE and the Law	13
	Introduction	*13*
	Teachers and unions	*15*
	School governors and the law	*15*
	School boards and the law	*16*
	Negligence	*16*
	Accident reports	*17*
	Safe Practice	17
	Supervision of students on teaching practice	*17*
	Supervision of pupils	*18*
	Sick notes	*19*
	Pupils with serious medical conditions	*19*
	Culture and clothing	*20*
	Assault courses	*20*
	Adventure playgrounds	*21*
	Outdoor climbing frames	*21*
	Maintenance of premises and equipment	*22*
	PE for Pupils with Special Educational Needs	23
	General	*23*
	Physical disabilities and conditions	*24*
	Mental disabilities	*27*
	Sensory impairment	*27*
	Pupils in wheelchairs	*27*

	Insurance	28
	First Aid	30

Part Two — Gymnastics and Dance — 33

- Gymnastics — 33
  - *General* — 33
  - *Teaching methods* — 33
  - *Learning of skills* — 34
  - *Pupil safety* — 35
  - *Safety of buildings* — 36
  - *Safety of apparatus* — 36
  - *Common faults in apparatus* — 37
- Dance — 40
  - *General* — 40
  - *Aerobics* — 40

Part Three — Swimming and Diving — 41

- Swimming — 41
- Diving — 43

Part Four — Games and Sports — 45

- Conduct and Supervision — 45
- Archery — 46
- Association Football — 49
- Athletics — 50
  - *Field events* — 51
  - *Track events* — 56
  - *Cross-country* — 56
- Basketball — 57
- Boxing — 58
- Cricket — 58
- Cycling — 59
- Fencing — 60
- Gaelic Sports — 62
- Golf — 62
- Hockey — 63
- Horse-riding — 64
- Judo — 65
- Lacrosse — 66
  - *Men's lacrosse* — 66
  - *Women's lacrosse* — 66

Martial Arts	67
Aikido	67
Karate	67
Kendo	68
Other martial arts	69
Netball	69
Racket Games	69
Rounders	71
Rowing	71
Rugby Union and Rugby League	72
Skating	73
Ice-skating	73
Roller-skating	73
Trampolining	74
Trampette activities	77
Volleyball	78
Weight Training	79
Weightlifting	80
Wrestling, Olympic-style	80

Part Five   Outdoor Pursuits   83

General	83
Teaching outdoor pursuits	84
Parental consent	85
Trips overseas	85
Camping	87
Canoeing	88
Caving and Potholing	91
Climbing and Mountain-walking	94
Rock-climbing	95
Orienteering	96
Sailing	97
Skiing	99
Sub-aqua Diving and Snorkelling	101
Outdoor Pursuits Not Included in This Book	103

Further Reading   **105**

Useful Addresses   **111**

Acknowledgements

The Association is deeply indebted to the many individuals who have given their time and energy by offering advice, revising drafts and supplying material for inclusion in this book.

Officers from many organisations, including national governing bodies of sport and schools' sports associations, have made significant contributions to this work on safety, and the Association offers its grateful thanks to them all.

The co-operation and contributions from Her Majesty's Inspectorate in Scotland, Northern Ireland, Wales and England have been invaluable.

Abbreviations Used in the Text

BAALPE	British Association of Advisers and Lecturers in Physical Education
BS	British Standard
DENI	Department of Education for Northern Ireland
DES	Department of Education and Science
EA	Education Authority (Scotland)
GM	Grant-maintained (school)
HSE	Health and Safety Executive
LEA	Local Education Authority (England and Wales)
LMS	Local Management of Schools
PE	Physical Education
SED	Scottish Education Department
SEN	Special Educational Needs

Introduction

The tragedies in recent years involving school parties at Lands End and in Austria have sharpened awareness of the importance of safety throughout education.

Nowhere in school life is this need for safe practice greater than in physical education (PE). PE is by its very nature a challenge to growing children, setting goals which in order to be met demand a mixture of skill, fitness and personal judgement. The risk of accident and injury is ever-present, but the ability to anticipate hazards and to minimise them can be developed early on in a PE teacher's career.

The purpose of this book is to advise on safe practice across the range of activities regularly included in PE, and where necessary to interpret statutory and case law, so that teachers can approach their daily work with confidence, learning from the accumulated wisdom of more experienced colleagues.

In England and Wales, changes in school management ushered in by the Education Reform Act 1988, and the emergence of new types of school such as grant-maintained (GM) schools, will devolve responsibility on governors and school staff for more of the day-to-day decisions on safety matters. LEA (local education authority) officials, PE advisers, school governors and headteachers are therefore urged to ensure that this book is available in all schools and colleges where PE is practised.

The advice in this publication on safe practice is also relevant in Scotland, where the provisions of the Health and Safety at Work (etc) Act 1974 apply as they do in England and Wales. However, Scotland has separate legislation relating to the provision of education. The main Acts are the Education (Scotland) Act 1980, the School Boards (Scotland) Act 1988 and the Self-governing Schools etc (Scotland) Act 1989. The system of school management in Scotland differs from that in England and Wales. References to "school governors" and "governing bodies" do not apply to education-authority schools in

Scotland. In Scotland reference is made to education authorities (EAs), not to local education authorities (LEAs).

This revised edition contains several new features, including:

- a checklist of common faults in gymnastics apparatus;
- points to look out for in the design and use of outdoor climbing frames;
- a consideration of the wider implications of special educational needs.

The book has relevance for primary schools, middle schools, secondary schools, community colleges and also the youth service. The National Curriculum is peculiar to England and Wales, but this edition has paid particular attention to the curricular and extra-curricular work in all four home countries. Reading lists and key addresses are also included.

HIV and AIDS

The implications of AIDS and the risks of HIV infection are of great concern within the whole of society. They should be considered carefully by *all* teachers, regardless of their specialist subject-area.

PE teachers, together with their colleagues in other departments, should consult the up-to-date advice issued by their LEA or EA and by the relevant government departments. If this advice is followed, any risk of HIV infection should be minimal.

Part One
PE, the Law and Safe Practice

Qualifications for Teaching PE

General
There is no law which requires that a teacher must hold a specific award before teaching any activity in PE. That said, LEAs and governing bodies of schools may establish their own policies and insist on certain minimum qualifications, particularly for the teaching of the more hazardous sports.

It is vital that anyone teaching hazardous sports is qualified by training and experience to handle the known, inherent dangers. Some teacher-training institutions, most LEAs and national sport governing bodies provide training courses in the teaching of these hazardous aspects of the PE programme. When these courses are completed, certificates may be awarded which indicate the level to which the recipients are regarded as competent to teach or coach the activity concerned. Such evidence can be of assistance to headteachers when considering a request for the introduction of a potentially hazardous activity in the PE programme.

It should be noted, however, that many of these qualifications have to be revalidated periodically in order to be of current value. Guidance relating to any such requirement is available from the LEA's PE adviser or from the governing body that provides the award.

Primary schools
Most teachers in primary schools will be required to teach the following aspects of the subject to an appropriate standard:

- gymnastics
- dance
- minor games and small-team versions of national major games
- swimming
- athletics.

Teachers with little or no initial training in PE run risks if they undertake to teach more than simple skills. Such teachers should be given appropriate in-service training before being allowed to present a full range of activities. Headteachers must be satisfied that all teachers who are required to teach PE are able to present the activities in a safe environment, and that they have an understanding of the needs and stages of development of all the children in their class.

Teachers should obtain the permission of the headteacher before introducing any new activity. This is particularly important if the activity is potentially hazardous. Some LEAs do not permit the use of certain items of equipment in primary schools (for example, rebound equipment such as trampolines and trampettes), and headteachers should ensure that they are aware of any such constraints.

In Scotland, PE may only be taught by those teachers who have covered the subject in their training course.

Secondary schools
Teachers who have responsibility for the planning and presentation of PE programmes in secondary schools should be qualified by initial training at an institute of higher education that is recognised by the DES as providing specialist courses for the teaching of PE. This basic qualification may need to be enhanced by in-service training in specific aspects of PE before the teacher can be regarded as suitably qualified to conduct the broad range of activities that is frequently presented in school programmes.

All specialist PE teachers in Scottish secondary schools must be registered with the General Teaching Council for Scotland.

As the curriculum widens further, some schools may include so-called *emergent* activities, for which codes of safe practice may still be in the process of formulation. Headteachers are advised to proceed with caution in such situations, and to contact both the national governing body of the sport and their own LEA adviser or insurers for the best advice available. It is also prudent to establish that adequate insurance cover is available in the unfortunate event of a serious accident to a pupil.

No teacher lacking experience and personal expertise in an emergent activity should take any responsibility for pupils engaging in that activity.

In Scotland there is a good match (99.5%) between the PE that is taught and the qualifications of the teachers who teach it. The education bodies there will continue to stress the importance of a specialised teaching qualification in PE.

Help from parents and other teachers

Teachers of other curriculum subjects, and volunteers (often parents), frequently help to teach or coach aspects of the PE programme, both within the curriculum and during extracurricular activities, and also at special events such as sports days. In England and Wales this is recognised as a regular and approved practice, and is of great benefit when there is a desire to extend the opportunities available to pupils.

It is vital, however, to ensure that these helpers are knowledgeable about the games or activities they are supervising, and that they have been briefed on their roles by the head of the PE department. They must be familiar with, and capable of enforcing, the established rules of the game or activity. When inexperienced staff or volunteers are engaged to assist at athletics competitions, they must not officiate alone at potentially hazardous events such as discus- or javelin-throwing.

The use of helpers or teachers with limited training or experience in the activity could leave the responsible governing body, LEA or headteacher open to an action for damages should a serious accident occur.

Further advice on the supervision of games is given at the beginning of **Part Four — Games and Sports**.

Recommended reading
- *Your Legal Position in Teaching*: pages 8–10
- *Headteacher's Legal Guide*: pages 3.9–3.13
- Health and Safety at Work etc Act 1974

For publication details, see **Further Reading** on page 105.

PE and the Law

Introduction

"He who would be his own lawyer has got a fool for a client." This book does not attempt to interpret the law. That said, experience gained from accidents that have led to court cases has often helped to shape good practice, and may also help in interpreting the law.

Common law and statute law impose general duties on individuals and bodies. Any breach of these duties which causes injury or loss may give rise to a claim for damages (compensation), or sometimes even to criminal penalties.

Under common law, all teachers are expected to act *in loco parentis*, exercising the same degree of responsibility for the pupils in their care as would any reasonably careful parent when looking after his or her own children. This so-called *duty of care* exists whenever a teacher is in

> Teachers in Scotland should pay particular attention to the School Boards (Scotland) Act 1988 and the Self-governing Schools etc (Scotland) Act 1989.

charge of pupils, whether or not the activity is part of the curriculum, and whether or not it takes place during school hours. Indeed, the duties of teachers in this regard will often go beyond what is normally expected of a parent. This is particularly true in the area of sporting and gymnastic activities, where teachers can be expected to be more fully aware of the potential dangers to pupils. This also applies during school journeys at home and abroad, and in the case of pupils who are 18 or 19 years of age, even though they are no longer regarded as minors.

Under statute law, responsibility for safety in LEA-maintained schools rests mainly with the LEAs; in voluntary-aided and GM schools it lies with the governing body; and in independent schools (including City Technology Colleges) it rests with the governing body or the proprietors.

In England and Wales, the professional duties of a teacher are currently set out in the School Teachers Pay and Conditions Document 1990, which by virtue of Section 3(6) of the Teachers Pay and Conditions Act 1987 has the same effect as if it had been incorporated in the contract of employment for every schoolteacher in an LEA-maintained primary or secondary school or GM school.

These duties include "maintaining good order and discipline among the pupils and safeguarding their health and safety both when they are authorised to be on the school premises and when they are engaged in authorised school activities elsewhere." (Paragraph 35(7))

The Health and Safety at Work etc Act 1974 is mainly concerned with the duties of an employer towards his employees. Section 1(3) of the Act imposes a general duty on every employer "to conduct his undertaking in such a way as to ensure, so far as is reasonably practicable, that persons not in his employment who may be affected thereby are not thereby exposed to risks to their health or safety." Such persons will include the pupils in a school. In a county or controlled school, the duty will rest with the LEA; in a voluntary-aided or GM school with the governing body; and in an independent school (including a City Technology College) it will normally rest with the proprietor. (There are appropriate parallels in Scotland.)

Section 2(3) of the Health and Safety at Work etc Act 1974 places a duty on every employer to prepare, and as often as may be appropriate revise, a written statement of his general policy with respect to the health and safety at work of his employees and the organisation and arrangements for the time being in force for carrying out that policy, and to bring the statement and any revision of it to the notice of all his employees.

Many LEAs have in practice drawn up working safety codes for PE, founded on good practice over the years. Regular and approved practice stems from these codes, which are regularly supplemented by head-teachers and PE advisers. Safe lessons can be planned within this framework, and beyond that all teachers must use their own judgement.

Further reference should be made to pages 3.2–3.5 of the *Headteacher's Legal Guide* (see **Further Reading**, page 105) for a typical safety policy statement of the kind that might be adopted by an LEA, together with an addendum dealing with the position in voluntary-aided schools.

Teachers and unions
All teachers should consider joining a teachers' union that offers legal help to its members. Any teacher involved in litigation should immediately contact his or her union for advice.

School governors and the law
Section 16(1) of the Education (No 2) Act 1986 (England and Wales) provides that:

"The articles of government for every county, voluntary and maintained special school shall provide for the conduct of the school to be under the direction of the governing body, but subject to any provision of the articles conferring specific functions on any person other than the governing body and to the provision made (otherwise than in the articles) by or under this Act or any other enactment."

The phased introduction of Local Management of Schools (LMS) in England and Wales from April 1990 in LEA-maintained schools will give school governors an even bigger say in the day-to-day running of schools. While the duties of the LEA as employers under the Health and Safety at Work etc Act 1974 will remain, a greater number of decisions having safety implications will be made at school level. School governors will, for example, be able to buy PE equipment and arrange for its maintenance without reference to the LEA.

School governing bodies should comply as closely as they can with the LEA's health and safety codes.

Governors are unlikely to incur personal liability for negligence under LMS if they have acted "in good faith" when exercising their powers. Therefore if a school follows the codes of safe practice in PE and the advice set out in this book, then its governors should have nothing to fear.

This advice applies equally to voluntary-aided and GM schools, where the governing body is responsible for the school premises and (as employer) for the staff. The DES requires GM school governing bodies to take out employers' and public-liability insurance cover.

In Scotland, the SED will require boards of management of self-governing schools (the equivalent of GM schools in England and Wales) to take out similar cover.

School boards and the law

School boards are established in EA schools in Scotland under the School Boards (Scotland) Act 1988. Their powers are significantly different from those of governing bodies in England and Wales. While school boards exercise basic powers and responsibilities, and have a general interest in the safety and welfare of pupils, the responsibility for health and safety matters in the school rests primarily with the EA and not with the school board. However, where school boards take on delegated functions from the EA relating to the school, then (depending on the nature of these functions) the school boards may have increased responsibilities with respect to health and safety. If school boards are in any doubt about their responsibilities, they should consult their EA.

Negligence

The standard of care required of a teacher has been expressed as that of "a reasonably prudent parent, judged not in the context of his own home but in that of a school".

A claim for damages on grounds of negligence will only succeed if it can be shown that there was negligence on the part of the teacher (or of any other employee) which has directly resulted in an injury to a pupil. The claim would normally be made by a parent or guardian against the LEA[1] or governing body on the grounds that they, as employers, were liable for the negligent acts of their employee.

It is most unusual for a teacher to be sued personally. If, however, damages are awarded against the LEA or governing body on account of the negligent acts of a teacher, then that teacher can be asked for a contribution towards the damages. But except in cases of gross negligence it is very rare for an LEA[1], governing body or its insurance company to exercise this right.

Defence against charges of negligence

Charges of negligence are very much easier to refute if it can be shown that:

- All reasonable steps had been taken to ensure the safety of premises and equipment.

---

1 In Scotland the self-governing school, technology academy, EA or school board.

- The class had been taught about the need for safety, and had been warned against foolhardiness in a manner appropriate to the pupils' age, intelligence and experience.

- The class had been systematically prepared for the activities being undertaken, and attention had been paid to footwear and clothing.

- The work, and the manner in which it was done, were in keeping with regular and approved practice in other schools in the country.

- Any local or overseas visits, outdoor pursuits or other occasional activities had proceeded with the prior agreement of parents by means of signed forms of consent. (Headteachers will normally draw up an appropriate consent form; see page 86.)

A much fuller explanation of a teacher's duty of care is given in *Teachers and the Law* by G. R. Barrell (see **Further Reading**, page 105).

Accident reports
When a pupil suffers serious injury, then by law the details must be reported immediately by telephone, and then within seven days on an official form, to the HSE, headteacher, LEA, EA, governing body or school board, giving:

- the date, time and place of the accident
- the name of the teacher in charge at the time
- the names of any witnesses.

It is helpful to the HSE, LEA or governing body to know how the accident occurred. Details about responsibility for the accident need not be given. If the teacher has any doubts about the facts, or considers the questions ambiguous, he or she should ask the headteacher for help.

Safe Practice

Supervision of students on teaching practice
The ultimate aim of teaching practice, in PE as in other subjects, is for the student to achieve a sufficient level of competence and experience to be able to take lessons that are not closely supervised. Throughout the practice it must always be remembered that students are not additional members of staff but are in training. They expect (and should receive) constructive help with regard to the preparation of lessons, teaching methods, the appropriateness of any materials to be used, organisational skills and professional conduct. All these factors will influence safe practice in their teaching.

It must be remembered that the regular teacher of the class always retains the duty-of-care responsibility for the pupils' safety.

The following arrangements are advised for the supervision of students on teaching practice:

- The student should make a preliminary visit to the school, during which as much information as possible should be given regarding what activities are expected to be taught. This will enable the preparation to be undertaken well in advance of the practice.

- A student engaged on his or her first teaching practice should eventually be allowed to take a complete lesson, provided that the responsible teacher is present throughout to provide direct support and supervision. Prior to the lesson, the teacher should be satisfied that the student is capable, and that the work to be attempted is appropriate to the age and development of the pupils.

- In the teaching of sports involving limited hazard, such as badminton or tennis, a more experienced student can be left alone for brief periods provided that the class is well disciplined and that the work to be undertaken is within the compass of the pupils and the skill of the student. The supervising teacher should be confident that the student is competent and can be allowed to work alone. If the teacher is in any doubt, the student's tutor should be consulted.

Colleges of education in Scotland require a qualified teacher to be present at all times.

A student's competence to teach an activity will be influenced by:

- personal ability and interest in the activity, or knowledge and experience of the activity;
- the number of hours of the PE course devoted to the activity;
- the amount of time devoted to preparation before the teaching practice;
- the number of opportunities the student has had to observe good and safe practice in schools.

All students should have been taught (and should understand) the emergency procedures taken by the school in the event of an accident.

Supervision of pupils
Whatever the system of supervision, all teachers must be able to fulfil the following requirements:

- The pupils should know what is expected of them.
- The size of any group should be modified according to the pupils' maturity, competence, intelligence and experience.

- Teachers in Scotland should refer to regulations on nationally agreed class sizes.

- Teachers should know about their pupils' needs and strengths. (A teacher's awareness of any disabilities or medical conditions has been critical in court cases involving charges of negligence.)

- Careful account should be taken when planning activities in which pupils may go out of sight, such as orienteering or cross-country.

- Teachers should know of any drug therapy which a pupil is undergoing, and its effects on sensory acuity (sharpness of perception) or motor control and coordination.

- Special safety precautions should be observed in the case of pupils who are inexperienced or immature, or who have disabilities or behavioural disorders, especially when determining the appropriate level and nature of the activity.

- Class numbers must always be checked. In at least two known court cases, a teacher was able to show from the register that the pupil in question was not even in the class at the time of the alleged incident. In swimming and cross-country, pupils must be counted at the start and finish of the activity.

- Young pupils should whenever possible be accompanied on journeys to and from matches played at venues other than their own school, and should otherwise be encouraged to travel as a group. Parental consent for long school journeys should always be obtained. When a group or individual has special needs, additional supervision or support may be needed.

For more specific advice on supervision during games lessons, see **Part Four — Games and Sports**.

Sick notes

Sick notes from parents should never be treated lightly. If there is any reasonable doubt about their authenticity, the teacher should make tactful enquiries. Firm, sensible and fair questioning should establish the truth.

A note stating that a pupil has a specific illness should be accepted. If the pupil does not recover after a certain time, the situation should be clarified by a letter from the school expressing concern for the child's well-being and asking for a medical report. If this brings no response from the parent, the school welfare service should be asked to investigate.

Pupils with serious medical conditions

It is most important that parents declare any serious medical conditions to the school. In turn, it is vitally important for all teaching staff, particularly PE teachers, to be in possession of all the information held by the school about a pupil's medical condition.

Pupils with certain medical conditions such as epilepsy, asthma or diabetes usually attend mainstream schools. Teachers must know who these pupils are and what their condition entails, particularly in the area of PE. Epilepsy and asthma, for example, can be aggravated by personal stress and excitement.

Participation in normal PE should be strictly according to medical advice. Clearance to take part is normally given if the condition is not severe and if the pupil can be relied on to recognise the symptoms preceding an attack.

For more detailed information regarding specific medical conditions, see the section on **Physical disabilities and conditions** on page 24.

Culture and clothing

A school's policy document should explain that in the interests of health and safety appropriate kit should be worn and all jewellery and other personal effects should be removed before a PE lesson. Acceptable kit is that which presents no risk of injury to the wearer or to other pupils.

Rules on safety should be clear and firmly applied. Should they conflict with acceptable cultural practices, a sensible compromise is often possible: bracelets, for example, could be secured by the use of sticky tape or sweat bands. However, a school should be satisfied that any dress requirement is necessary and objectively justifiable, lest it should constitute unlawful racial discrimination.

Agencies for liaison with families can assist in helping parents and children to understand and cooperate. The support of local community leaders can also help.

Assault courses

Parents should be informed well in advance of any plans to use assault courses, and their written permission should be obtained for their child to take part (see pages 85–6).

The following precautions are essential:

- The teacher must check the course before use, and must decide whether any of the obstacles should be omitted, bearing in mind the age, abilities and general fitness of the class.

- Only pupils capable of meeting the physical demands of the course should take part.

- Strict supervision must be exercised, and any competitive element must be avoided.

Adventure playgrounds

- Playgrounds should be constructed by a specialist firm.
- The teacher or resident warden should ensure that all the apparatus is in working condition before play begins.
- If the playground is used for voluntary attendance outside school hours, the equipment must be checked carefully at least once a day.
- Constant supervision is vital.
- Pupils need to be continually reminded:
    - to think before they do anything;
    - to respect the needs of others, and to give them enough space, especially when making swinging movements;
    - to recognise faulty apparatus, especially where fraying and chafing may weaken ropes and wire cables, and to report this immediately.

Outdoor climbing frames

Care is needed in selecting the most suitable type of outdoor climbing frame, but even more care is needed in supervising its use. The pupils' natural agility should not be inhibited, but at the same time they must be protected from their own tendency to take risks. Supervision must be provided at all times.

Design and siting

- Professionally designed equipment is recommended. Improvised equipment should be approved by the LEA or school governors before being used.
- Long, low frames are generally better than high ones: 2.5 m (8 ft) is the maximum suitable height.
- Working surfaces should offer good grip for hands and feet to climb on, the only exception being the so-called slide and roll surfaces.
- The diameter of any tube that is to be gripped should be appropriate to the hand size of the children who use the frame.
- Frames designed to offer safe escape systems are better than those with precipitate drops.
- Frames should be sited away from other structures, and where they can most easily be supervised.
- The surrounding surface should be non-slip and uniform.

Safer surfaces There has been a great effort in recent years to install impact-absorbent surfaces below outdoor climbing frames, especially in public parks, where supervision is usually less thorough than in schools. However, there is no surface as yet which will prevent head injury or fracture when a child falls from a height greater than one metre (40 in). Such injuries are more affected by the angle of impact than by the shock-absorbent qualities of the surface. Other factors which influence the extent of any injury include the child's weight and skeletal structure.

Concrete should not be used for playground surfaces. Where any unsupervised play takes place, the surface should be in accordance with the British Standard specification BS 5696 Part 3 (1979) Section 4.2.

Teacher supervision
- Staff must be familiar with the apparatus and with the abilities of the pupils.
- Both staff and pupils need to know the maximum number that can safely use the frame at any one time.
- Pupils must wear safe footwear that provides good traction between foot and frame; smooth soles are dangerous.
- Small children, especially those at nursery level, should not use the apparatus at the same time as older pupils. Separate break times or playtimes will achieve this.
- Frames should not be used in bad weather.

Ancillaries and volunteer helpers If a headteacher decides that outdoor apparatus can be used at break times and playtimes, and employs ancillary staff for supervisory duties, then these should be paid employees of the LEA or governing body. If volunteer helpers are used, they should not be placed in sole charge, and in either case the headteacher should ensure that they clearly understand their duties.

Maintenance of premises and equipment
Vigilance is essential when checking the condition of premises and equipment to be used for PE, as defects can develop in the intervals between annual inspections. Any defect should be reported to the headteacher, and the equipment should be taken out of use until it has been repaired. Premises and equipment are subject to the Health and Safety at Work etc Act 1974 (Building Regulations for Schools).

Moreover, care should be taken, even with well-maintained premises, that they do not cause a hazard to pupils. For example, a highly polished floor may be too dangerous for certain activities without the use of mats. The aim should be to ensure that the general conditions are safe for the conduct of PE, and that all risks are avoided that can be reasonably foreseen.

In primary schools, one teacher should be specifically responsible for the condition and availability of PE equipment. In secondary schools, this responsibility should be clearly allocated.

Apparatus and equipment should be carefully stored, preferably in a separate space, and pupils should be encouraged to report any defects they see. (See later sections for more specific advice, particularly with regard to British Standards.)

PE for Pupils with Special Educational Needs

General

The Education Act 1981 placed a duty on LEAs, subject to certain conditions, to integrate children with special educational needs (SEN) into mainstream schools. The result was that by 1989 over 47,000 children with statements of SEN[1] were being taught in ordinary schools, either in ordinary or in special classes. Thus both primary and secondary PE teachers may well find such pupils in their classes.

In such cases a special kind of teaching expertise and the right degree of caring is required. Just as a normal parent will devote extra care to a child with these needs, so then should the teacher. Yet at the same time the child should not be protected to the point of stifling development.

Points to consider Any teacher in charge of a pupil with SEN must know:

- the nature of the child's learning problem, disability, or emotional or behavioural disorder;
- any constraints on physical activity as a result of the disability or of any required medication.

Such problems might include:

- poor coordination or balance
- lack of spatial concept or perception
- slow reaction times
- variable levels of concentration
- cardiovascular inhibition
- muscle spasms
- sensory loss.

---

[1] Not all these children have a mental or physical disability: children with dyslexia, for example, are also classified as having SEN.

The learning procedure must be slowed down, and the pupil must be able to indicate that he or she understands the instructions given.

If hazardous activities are taught, smaller classes or even one-to-one tuition may be required. The same applies when pupils with locomotion or incontinence problems have to use showers or follow specific cleansing procedures.

In the case of any child with physical, medical or sensory difficulties, it is essential to consult other professionals before embarking on a PE programme. Those consulted should include the child's parents, doctor, and possibly physiotherapist. Any medical information on the child that is not contained in school records can be obtained through school nurses.

While certain safety factors need to be considered, these children need a physical programme even more than ordinary children because of the more protected sedentary life they often lead.

Physical disabilities and conditions

Where pupils have physical disabilities, it is vital to note the following points:

- Children with physical disabilities do not form a homogeneous group.

- A physical disability means that physical exercise is all the more essential.

- A pupil's doctor and/or physiotherapist must be consulted before he or she takes part in PE. Once this medical advice has been obtained, then a full and meaningful programme of activity can be provided.

- The teacher must be aware of any medication that such children might be taking, and whether there are any side effects.

- Physical support should be available if required, either from the teacher or from a fellow-pupil. Such support will be absolutely necessary in some activities, but independence should be encouraged in as many activities as possible.

- The teacher should be able to assess confidently whether the child should continue with an activity, and whether he or she has understood an instruction.

Epilepsy Before a pupil with epilepsy can take part in PE, the matter must be cleared in writing both by the family doctor and by the parents, specifying the extent to which participation is to be permitted.

The teacher should also know how to deal with an epileptic fit.

Gymnastics Children subject to fits should not be allowed to go high up on climbing apparatus. Low-level apparatus should always be provided that offers similar challenges.

It is also advisable to use the buddy system when using apparatus in the gym.

Swimming A child with epilepsy should be paired with a strong swimmer, using the buddy system. There should always be a competent lifesaver on the pool side who can hold a child's head above the water if a fit occurs.

The advice of the British Epilepsy Association is that a person known to suffer from epilepsy should be allowed to swim provided that:

- the person's doctor has given full approval;
- the person is accompanied in the water by a strong swimmer, preferably a lifesaver;
- both swimmers are watched by a third person on the pool side.

Some further advice is given under **Swimming** (see page 42).

Further information Further information and advice concerning physical activity for those with epilepsy is contained in the *Health Education Project Newsletter* No 25 (May 1990), which is obtainable from the Physical Education Association (see **Useful Addresses**, page 111).

Asthma Pupils who suffer breathing problems during a PE lesson will normally know how to cope with these themselves, but teachers should be familiar with the procedures to be taken if the symptoms become more serious.

- Children should be encouraged to cope with their attacks, and especially to exhale in the event of an attack.
- Children should be encouraged to carry their inhalers.
- Some children may need to take medication before vigorous physical exercise.
- Prolonged strenuous exercise such as cross-country should be avoided.
- A sensible and thorough warm-up is particularly essential for asthmatics.
- Swimming is beneficial, but overheated or underheated pools should be avoided.

Further information Further and more detailed advice regarding physical activity for those with asthma is available from the National Asthma Campaign, and is also contained in the *Health Education Project Newsletter* No 24 (March

1990), which is obtainable from the Physical Education Association (see **Useful Addresses**, page 111).

Diabetes The main potential danger for diabetics is when the level of sugar (glucose) in the blood falls too low during exercise.

It is therefore important to check that all diabetic pupils have made the necessary adjustments before strenuous exercise, such as altering their insulin injection or regulating their food intake. It is also advisable to have sources of extra carbohydrate available, such as bite-size chocolate bars.

The doctor may advise against PE immediately after lunch, when the blood-sugar level is low.

Further information Further and more detailed advice regarding physical activity for those with diabetes is available from the British Diabetic Association, and is also contained in the *Health Education Project Newsletter* No 24 (March 1990), which is obtainable from the Physical Education Association (see **Useful Addresses**, page 111).

Brittle bones Some children have a condition which means that their bones fracture easily. Contact sports should therefore be completely avoided. Swimming, however, is ideal provided that care is taken on entering and leaving the pool. These children need space, and crowded changing rooms and playgrounds should be avoided.

Cerebral palsy The child's physiotherapist must be consulted. Care must be taken to avoid any injury that may result from lack of sensation in the limbs. Fast movements may encourage bad movement patterns and provoke spasms. Loud noises may affect the child's behaviour.

Heart defects It is essential to have written medical advice as to which activities are permissible. These children should never be allowed to become cold.

Still's disease (juvenile arthritis) It is essential to seek advice from the child's parents and physiotherapist before any physical activity is undertaken. Because of stiffness and pain in the joints, the child may require more time for general movement. Swimming should be encouraged as it removes weight-bearing loads.

Spina bifida Treatment will depend on where the lesion is, but any resulting paralysis means that care is needed to avoid injury in the lower limbs. This is extremely important in swimming pools.

Mental disabilities

For pupils with mental disabilities, the teaching process will need to be slowed down and restructured so that the pupil understands each task and can recognise achievements.

Sensory impairment

For pupils with impaired sensory systems such as sight or hearing, the teacher must know the kind of support needed for the initial learning experience, and when and how to withdraw that support.

Sight problems

- It is essential for sight-impaired children to become independent as soon as possible.

- All apparatus and equipment must be stored consistently and always in the same place. Support will be needed to guide the child to feel the pieces of equipment and their relationship to each other. The texture of the apparatus is important.

- Allowances should be made for the fact that many children may be well behind their peers as a result of lack of experience.

Swimming

- Medical clearance for swimming is essential, as chlorinated water may damage the eyes. Goggles may be helpful in giving protection.

- The buddy system is desirable.

- An easily identifiable cap may be necessary in crowded pools.

- Diving is undesirable unless the doctor's consent has been given.

- Ropes or helpers are necessary to prevent heads being bumped on the sides of the pool.

Hearing problems

- Before any physical activity is undertaken, clear methods of communication should be established between the teacher and the pupil.

- Teaching methods may need to be modified, especially in the area of demonstration and manipulation.

- In swimming the use of the buddy system is essential.

- Short, slow instructions are necessary.

Pupils in wheelchairs

Teachers and helpers should understand the problems associated with the use of wheelchairs.

The following points should be considered:

- Sports and racing wheelchairs should be adapted to each individual pupil and to the demands of the activity. They should also be checked for stability.
- Participation in throwing events from a wheelchair demands good anchorage below the pupil's centre of gravity. The use of a holding device is recommended. Otherwise it may be necessary for an adult to hold the chair while the throw is executed.
- Footrests should be at the correct level so that the feet are well supported and neither feet nor legs are at risk of injury from other chairs.
- Tyres, wheels and brakes should be subject to regular checks and repairs.
- Pupils should not be strapped into wheelchairs except at the side of a swimming pool.
- Sport and racing wheelchairs should be checked to make sure they are mechanically safe and sound.
- Calf straps must be used when racing.
- Where cushions are used, these should be well fitting, and should be checked to make sure they do not impede the movement of the wheelchair.
- Pupils should not stand on the footrests.
- Regular maintenance is essential.
- A strap of webbing or leather at least 5 cm (2 in) wide must be attached to each of the telescopic uprights of the footrest. This strap must be positioned so as to ensure that the feet cannot fall off, touch the ground or get caught in the wheels.
- Teachers and helpers should be aware of the individual needs of pupils when getting into and out of the wheelchair, and should be able to help as necessary.

Further reading For details of recommended reading on special educational needs, see **Further Reading**, page 105.

Insurance

After taking account of nationally accepted regular and approved practice in PE, some LEAs or governing bodies set out their own codes of practice designed to reduce the risk of litigation on grounds of negligence, and to provide guidelines which may reduce the occurrence of accidents. Such codes vary considerably, and this may affect the insurance cover that is offered regarding:

- the use of minibuses;
- the use of teachers' own cars to take pupils to extracurricular activities organised by the school;
- parental assistance given to PE teachers in and out of school hours;
- the conduct of school, county and national sports championships.

Headteachers and heads of PE departments must ensure that all teachers and volunteer helpers are fully aware of liability and insurance arrangements.

Most LEAs and governing bodies of schools accept that properly planned events at local, national and international level are of benefit to pupils. They therefore indemnify their teachers, and pay compensation up to specified limits in the event of an accident occurring when the teachers voluntarily participate in these activities outside the scope of their contract of service.

However, the terms of such indemnities differ from case to case. Some, for example, exclude certain hazardous activities such as skiing, rock-climbing, caving, potholing and white-water canoeing, or activities that take place abroad. It is essential, therefore, for teachers to check the precise terms of the indemnity offered so as to ensure that it affords them adequate protection.

Teachers are deemed to be acting of their own free will if they take part in an activity run by a regional or national body which has no connection with their school or with other schools in their LEA. In such circumstances a teacher is well advised to check that his or her participation in the event is covered by a suitable indemnity issued by the organising body, or by insurance taken out by that body.

Insurance for personal injury

LEAs and governing bodies do not normally provide personal accident cover for pupils or employees who are injured while taking part in organised activities. There is therefore no immediate or automatic compensation for such injuries. That said, some insurance companies now offer special schemes covering most activities provided normally in PE. Headteachers are advised to inform parents as to the availability of these schemes. Teachers should be aware of any limitations on the insurance cover provided by their employer, and should consider taking out additional cover.

Motor insurance

If an LEA or governing body asks its teachers to use their own private cars to transport pupils to and from fixtures, then that body may assist with the financial cost of insurance cover. It is more usual, however, for teachers to meet the cost themselves. It is then the teachers' responsibility to make sure that their car-insurance policies allow for this.

Insurers should be asked to approve any such use of the car, and the LEA or governing body should be informed of the arrangements.

Insurance cover for area and district meetings Local school sports associations, and organisers of school, youth and club events, should check both their own policies and those arranged through their LEA to ensure that the appropriate indemnity, personal-accident and public-liability insurance cover has been arranged. Voluntary helpers such as parents should be covered, as well as officials and teachers.

If organisers are unsure of whether their existing policies provide sufficient cover, they are strongly advised to make separate arrangements to extend it.

First Aid

General Accident prevention is always the PE teacher's first safety consideration, but in emergencies the same teacher should be able to care for the injured person without causing further complications.

First aid is defined as the immediate and sustained care given to the victim of a sudden illness or accident until more professional help becomes available. It is often as important to know what *not* to do as to know what should be done.

Qualifications PE teachers are advised to take the full first-aid certificate course provided by the St John Ambulance Brigade, the St Andrew's Ambulance Association or the British Red Cross Society. The names of all teachers who are thus qualified should be known to all members of staff.

In large PE departments, at least one teacher should hold a current certificate. If this is not possible, then teachers should acquire the knowledge and skills outlined below, both by reading and by attendance at shorter courses.

If at all practicable, pupils should also be trained in first aid; the St John Ambulance Brigade, the St Andrew's Ambulance Association and the British Red Cross Society often provide help with this, as do local ambulance stations.

Swimming Teachers involved with swimming should be aware of the need to update their qualifications every three years. The ASA/RLSS Teachers Certificate is an appropriate alternative to the more exacting Pool Bronze Medallion (see also **Further Reading**, page 106).

Knowledge All PE teachers should know how to:

- perform cardiopulmonary and expired-air resuscitation (external chest compression and mouth-to-mouth ventilation);[1]
- cope initially with fractures, shock, burns, bruises, grazes, bleeding, scalds, bites, stings, excessive heat, and hypothermia;
- treat a severe haemorrhage;
- decide whether an injured pupil should be moved;
- decide when to leave to the experts more serious injuries such as fractures, spinal injuries or dislocations;
- use the life-saving equipment available at swimming pools, which may take the form of recovery aids or advanced resuscitation equipment.

Medical conditions Teachers must also know the medical conditions which may cause problems (see page 24), such as diabetes, epilepsy, allergies and asthma. An up-to-date register should be kept with medical information on all pupils, and this should be consulted whenever hospital treatment is required.

Priorities When an accident occurs, the aims are to save life, to help recovery and to avoid complications. Teachers should follow this nine-point plan:

1 Take charge, keep calm, get others to help.

2 Assess the situation, work quietly and without fuss.

3 Give reassurance to the rest of the party.

4 Deal with any life-threatening situation first (for example, arrested breathing, bleeding or fractures).

5 Deal with the more serious injuries next.

6 If several people are injured, deal with those who will benefit most from immediate treatment.

7 Watch out for cases of shock.

8 If hospital treatment may be needed, do not give the patient drugs, drinks or food.

9 If in any doubt, call an ambulance.

Equipment One teacher in any school or PE department should take responsibility for ensuring that first-aid equipment is maintained ready for use. All staff

---

[1] This should be practised on a regular basis, at least annually.

and pupils should know where the equipment is, and should have access to the telephone numbers of the nearest doctor and casualty department.

The minimum contents of a first-aid box should be:

- several triangular cotton bandages
- safety pins
- a mild antiseptic solution
- a packet of sterilised gauze
- packets of sterilised cotton wool
- bandages of various sizes
- plasters of various sizes
- blunt-nosed scissors
- a crêpe bandage
- tweezers
- a pair of disposable gloves
- disposable resuscitation gauze.

Polythene exposure bags and inflatable splints are useful extra items for activities in open country.

Further reading   For details of recommended reading on first-aid procedures, see **Further Reading**, page 106.

Part Two
Gymnastics and Dance

Gymnastics

General

Gymnastics has evolved considerably over the years, and now takes several distinct forms, including Olympic and rhythmic gymnastics. These forms require both technical skill and precision, and place heavy demands on both teacher and pupil alike. All are therefore potentially hazardous. Teachers must ensure that both they and their pupils are aware of these hazards and take the necessary precautions.

Any member of staff taking gymnastics must be trained or qualified to teach the subject safely. Headteachers are responsible for checking the competence of teachers and helpers.

General precautions can be listed, but every hall, gymnasium, school and club has its own unique features. Headteachers, PE teachers and coaches are advised to add specific rules which apply to their own facilities.

At any inquiry following a gymnastics accident, concern is always expressed about the size and ability of a class in relation to the activity being undertaken.

Teaching methods

Two methods of teaching gymnastics are normally found in schools. They are generally known as the *indirect* and the *direct* approach.

The indirect approach The indirect approach caters for the needs and abilities of all pupils, and allows them to approach the exercises that have been set in their own way.

Since run-up, take-off, flight and landing are not usually predictable, it is almost impossible to use a system of catching and standing by. A measure of predictability is only possible when a pupil sets out to reproduce the pattern of a previously performed movement. The teacher should be aware of this point, and when the attempted movement is particularly challenging, the teacher should ensure that the pupil has a reasonable chance of success.

When appropriate, the teacher may also give active encouragement and help to individual pupils. The teacher and pupil should then discuss the sequence of the movement concerned, ensuring that the mechanics are understood. Any interesting problems should be demonstrated to the entire class, together with their solutions.

The indirect approach increases pupils' self-awareness, but this should not be allowed to develop into selfishness. Pupils should be taught to be cooperative and courteous.

The direct approach   The direct approach covers the formal teaching and coaching of specific disciplines such as the vault. It involves the use of equipment such as vaulting horses, beams and bars.

This approach should only be used by a teacher or coach with a qualification recognised by the LEA or governing body and with the appropriate teaching experience. The teacher or coach must fully understand the mechanics of each discipline and of the progressions leading up to it, and must also know the symptoms of physiological and psychological fatigue. The pupils' mental and physical readiness must be assessed before each new skill is taught.

The teacher or coach should attend appropriate in-service training courses from time to time in order to reinforce knowledge and learn about new developments.

Since the pattern of movement is predictable, the teacher must be ready to stand by and give support throughout. Pupils may be taught to give support to others, but only when the instructor is confident of their ability.

Vigilance is vital during vigorous swinging or circling movements, when premature or late release from the apparatus can occur.

Overhead rigs and other specialist aids should be used by pupils only under the direction of an experienced teacher or coach.

Learning of skills
Pupils learning a new skill should have the necessary strength, flexibility and body awareness, and should have passed through the progressive stages leading up to that new skill.

Good communication is essential between the teacher or coach and the pupil, together with a clear understanding of their respective responsibilities.

Skills learned earlier may have to be relearned after periods of inactivity such as holidays, or as a result of physiological changes occurring during growth and adolescence.

Pupil safety

Discipline Firm discipline is essential at all times. Sweets or gum should never be chewed during a class.

Warm-up A suitably graded warm-up should precede the main part of every class.

Clothing and personal effects
- Clothing should allow unrestricted movement without being loose.
- Tops for trampolining should have long sleeves to prevent friction burns to the forearms when performing activities such as front drops.
- Extra clothing may be worn for warm-ups.
- All jewellery and other personal effects such as watches should be removed, and long hair should be tied back.
- Handguards may be worn when gripping apparatus, particularly bars.
- On certain pieces of apparatus such as the parallel bars, moderate amounts of soft chalk (magnesium carbonate) should be used to give a safe grip.

Footwear Gymnastics should be performed either in purpose-designed gymnastics footwear, gym shoes or bare feet. For classes involving frequent high-velocity landings or rope climbing, footwear is kinder to the feet.

Footwear should be pliant and close-fitting, with enough serrations (or an equivalent feature) on the sole to give good traction. Trainers with hard plastic soles give poor traction and should not be worn.

On trampolines and trampettes, footwear with soft soles is appropriate provided that it gives sufficient traction. Woollen socks (but not other types) are a possible alternative. Bare feet should not be allowed because of the risk of injuries to the feet.

"Pirates" "Pirates" and other chasing games using apparatus as obstacles are dangerous and should never be played.

High-flight rotational skills Skills such as the long-arm overswing from a vaulting box or high table are hazardous and should not be attempted by novices. The same applies to forward rolls on landing: inexperienced pupils should be trained instead to make a controlled landing on two feet.

Safety of buildings

Cracked or broken windows must be replaced immediately with the type of glass appropriate to the teaching space.

Lights must be guarded if they are not impact-resistant. Socket outlets should be recessed and of a suitable design.

Main access doors should have some form of closure control. This is especially important on exposed, windy sites so as to minimise the risk of doors slamming unexpectedly.

Good ventilation is important throughout the academic year, and specialist professional advice should be sought on this.

Hygiene All PE premises, especially the floors, should be kept as clean as possible, and teachers should insist on high standards of tidiness.

Floors Floors should be smooth and non-slip, and should be cleaned in accordance with the LEA's instructions. Polish can be dangerous if used wrongly on gymnasium or hall floors. Wooden floors should be checked from time to time for splinters.

Wet patches on floors are a hazard. They are sometimes caused by leaking from flat roofs or windows, or by condensation resulting from temperature imbalance in cold weather.

Safety of apparatus

The teacher or coach should take the following precautions:

- Apparatus must conform to the standards of the British Standards Institution, and should be overhauled by a professional maintenance firm at least once a year.

- Insecure or broken apparatus should be removed from the working area and clearly marked as unfit for use.

- Apparatus should be assembled and dismantled systematically. It should be checked immediately before use, should be adequately spaced out, and should be adjusted to meet the needs of individuals. Pupils of all ages should take part in this process, and should be taught to report any loose fittings or wrong adjustments immediately.

- Fixed or portable equipment should not be used as obstacles for competitive games, especially where speed is involved.

- Runways should be straight and unobstructed.

Improvised apparatus Only apparatus that has been officially provided or approved should normally be used in PE. In most cases this will have been designed to give maximum stability. Any improvised equipment, such as is sometimes used in adventure playgrounds, should be checked for suitability and stability by a PE adviser or equipment officer before being brought into service. Chairs should never be used as PE equipment.

Mats The following points should be considered:

- Matting of sufficient size and density should be placed wherever a landing or dismount may occur, whether by accident or design.

- Mats should be stable, easy to clean, and light enough for pupils to handle. Surfaces should be free of holes or tears, and of concealed pins or stones.

- The one-inch (25-mm) general-purpose mat is adequate for most dismounts, and for cushioning the body in an easy rolling movement.

- Thicker mats should be used where greater protection is needed. The force of the landing is increased in the case of heavier participants.

- The mat should not produce excessive recoil. Recoil can cause serious stress on joints, especially the ankles, and can cause the gymnast to fall and exacerbate any injury. Some mats are specially designed to cope with high-impact landings without generating recoil.

- The core substances should be checked regularly to ensure that they are not disintegrating to the point where the mat no longer cushions landings.

- Where possible, only fire-resistant mats should be used. Some foams which have received fire-retardancy treatment lose their resilience and impact-absorption qualities more quickly than untreated materials. Regular checks of these newer materials are essential.

- High-jump landing beds should not be used in gymnastics.

- Where possible mats should be stored flat so as to present the smallest possible vertical surface area up which flames could travel. (Teachers at educational establishments in Northern Ireland are advised to refer to the DENI Circular 1989/21/27:1:89.)

Common faults in apparatus

A checklist such as the following should be drawn up for use by the teacher responsible:

Fixed apparatus

Hinged-type apparatus fixed to a wall

Check that:

- Bracing wires are stable and are not fraying at points of frictional contact.
- Castors are well oiled, and the contact surface is free from grit.
- Sockets in the floor are free from sweeping compound and other dirt.
- Locking nuts have not loosened.
- Any securing bolts are firmly fixed to their base.
- Any securing bolts fixing the apparatus to the wall have not worked loose over the years.
- Any wooden components are free from cracks or splinters.

Single and double beams

Ensure that:

- The hauling cables are free from rust and have not frayed.
- The trackway is oiled frequently so that the upright post runs smoothly.
- The beams are free from cracks and the shackle pins are firmly located on the hauling wires.
- There are sufficient pins and wedges.
- The floor sockets are free from obstructions, and the bolts fit well into the sockets.
- The beams move up and down smoothly.

Climbing ropes and other suspension apparatus

Check that:

- The drag lines are not worn, and there is a securing cleat to stabilise the ropes.
- The runway operates smoothly.
- No rope is knotted.
- The leather caps are not worn or missing, and their stitching is not working loose.
- The securing nuts are tight.

Portable apparatus

Free-standing folding apparatus (trestles)

Check that the horizontal stays are placed sufficiently wide apart to avoid the risk of a hand or foot getting trapped between them.

Vaulting apparatus Ensure that:

- The wood is free from splinters, and the covers are free from tears (leather covers should be rough and not highly polished through age or excessive use).
- There are no cracks or loose screws.
- Any height-adjustment mechanism works smoothly.
- All rubber stops are firmly fixed and in good condition, and no screws are in contact with the floor.
- Where sections interlock, such as with boxes, the angular interlocking surfaces are not rounded through use, allowing dangerous movement in the apparatus when struck during a vault.
- Any wheeling system works efficiently, and the wheels are off the floor when the equipment is in use.

Balance benches Check that:

- The bench is not warped, and the rubber buffers on the top are in place and make contact with the floor when the bench is inverted.
- The fixing hooks are properly covered with leather or rubber, and the screws are firm.
- The bracing brackets on the legs are firm.
- There are no splinters.
- The rubber pads at the bottom of the legs will protect the floor effectively.

Beating boards and springboards Check that:

- There are no cracks in the beating board, springboard or supports.
- The take-off surface is free of splinters and is smooth but non-slip.

Trampolines and trampettes See pages 75 and 77.

Scrambling nets Check that:

- The ropes are not wearing, and all fixing devices are secure.
- The nets are stabilised at all four corners so that there is no unexpected movement.

Planks Ensure that:

- There are no splinters.
- Any rubber protection pads or locking devices are in good condition.

Dance

General

Teachers of dance should be qualified or experienced, and should know about the structure and functioning of the human body. Aerobics, "pop-mobility" and other styles can place heavy demands on students, and may be harmful if incorrectly taught.

An adequate warm-up is essential before strenuous exercise. Care must be taken to ensure that all pupils are properly prepared for the physical demands of a lesson.

The following points should be stressed in any training programme for teachers of dance:

- Severe and/or uneven physical stress can cause damage to cartilages.

- Exercises performed too quickly may cause excessive stretching of the ligaments and loss of elasticity.

- Joints should never be moved beyond their normal range of movement.

- Excessive jogging or jumping on hard floors may cause jarring.

- Teachers should observe students carefully to check that they do not overexert themselves either physically or mentally, and that the correct body position is maintained.

- The following movements should be avoided: vigorous circular head movements; back-arching; kneeling; flat-back exercises.

Aerobics

This approach to cardiovascular (heart/lung) fitness development is already popular with the public, and is now finding favour in secondary-school PE regimes.

- Each pupil's ability should be individually assessed before classes begin, and the pupil should be appropriately paced using graded routines.

- Pupils should understand the principles of aerobics before starting work.

- Progress towards fitness results from a gradual increase in working time and exercise loads. Pupils should be taught to recognise the onset of fatigue, and to withdraw from the session as soon as this happens. "Burning off the fat" is not a realistic target for most pupils.

- Pupils should not be asked to adopt awkward postures if these result in pain.

Part Three
Swimming and Diving

Swimming

Responsibility for safety

From leaving the classroom until returning, the duty of care in swimming lessons remains with the teacher.

LEAs often engage instructors to help teachers with swimming lessons. A good working relationship between teacher and instructor is vital. The degree to which the instructor takes the initiative will depend on the teacher's expertise and experience, and should be arranged between them. Throughout the lesson, however, the teacher is responsible for monitoring the progress of the pupils, whether he or she is directing the session or not.

By law, anyone who makes premises available to non-employees must take all reasonable measures to ensure that the premises are safe and present no risk to health. This applies equally when schools use swimming pools belonging to other schools, or when school pools are used by outside agencies, groups or individuals. In all cases where the pool is being used for the teaching of swimming, it is regarded by law as a *place of work*.

In the case of pupils with serious medical conditions such as epilepsy, medical clearance and the written permission of parents are both essential before they can be allowed to take part in normal school swimming programmes (see pages 19 and 24–5).

Safety qualifications

Whenever there are pupils in the water, an adult must be present at the pool side who is able to effect a rescue and carry out cardiopulmonary resuscitation (see page 31).

The teaching certificates awarded by the Amateur Swimming Association and the Swimming Teachers' Association are both desirable qualifications for swimming teachers, but it should be remembered that these do not aim to guarantee up-to-date life-saving competence.

The supervision of activities such as canoeing (see page 88) or scuba diving (see page 101) requires specialist knowledge and training.

Supervision

- When more than 20 pupils are in the water at any one time, at least two adults should be present at the pool side to supervise.

- The teacher or instructor should be able to see all the pupils and the pool bottom throughout the lesson (glare from reflected light may be a problem in pools with a large expanse of glass).

- The teacher or instructor should not enter the water if this leaves no supervising adult at the pool side, except in emergencies or when the class is assembled at the pool side while the teacher is demonstrating a particular point.

- Pupils should be taught to report any mishap to the teacher or instructor; they should also work in pairs to check on each other's well-being.

- The class must be counted both before and after the lesson.

- Changing rooms must be adequately supervised.

Pupils with SEN and medical conditions

In the case of pupils with SEN, the class size should be reduced to take account of the pupils' age, intelligence and experience. Shallow-depth learner pools are much easier to supervise than large public pools. The presence of the public can be a problem. The help of other adults such as responsible parents is very useful.

Pupils with epilepsy should stay in shallow water unless working alongside a responsible person. Shimmering or flickering light reflected from the water may trigger an attack.

For more detailed advice on SEN, see the relevant section on page 23.

Pupil behaviour and swimwear

- An emergency drill to clear the pool should be practised regularly, and should be effected by means of an agreed signal such as a whistle or other audible warning.

- Pupils should never chew sweets or gum during a lesson, or be allowed to run on the pool surrounds.

- Many swimming-pool supervisors insist that long hair is covered by a bathing cap. No jewellery should be worn during swimming and diving.

- When goggles and masks are used, they should not be made of glass or breakable plastic; pupils should be taught to remove them by slipping them off the head rather than by stretching the retaining band.

- If for cultural or religious reasons pupils are allowed into the water in clothing other than usual swimwear, they should be restricted to shallow water until they have shown that they are able to swim competently. Liaison with community leaders can do much to minimise any problems.

Pool safety and equipment
- Adequate life-saving equipment, buoyancy aids and first-aid equipment, including a blanket, should be immediately to hand.
- There should be a telephone giving direct contact from the pool to the emergency services.
- Pool depths should be clearly indicated on the walls, and teachers should explain their significance, especially to beginners. All signs must conform to Part 1 of BS 5378, 1980. (Further details are given in *A Guide to the Safety Signs Regulations*; see **Further Reading**, page 106.)
- A pool divider, normally a rope, is useful for delineating shallow from deep water.
- A pool should not be used unless and until the water is sufficiently clear to enable the bottom of the pool to be visible at all depths.
- The doors to a school pool should be locked when the pool is not in use.

Pool temperatures Pupils learn to swim more quickly in comfortable temperatures. The most suitable water temperature is around 20°C, with an air temperature of one degree higher to avoid excess condensation. If the water is colder than usual for any reason, the lesson time should be reduced.

Diving

General Diving by its very nature can be dangerous, so a few simple but effective safety measures should be observed:

- Diving sessions should be supervised by a teacher or coach.
- Pupil numbers should be small enough to allow the teacher to watch all the divers. Pupils should be given room to practise.
- The water must be deep enough to avoid any possible danger of impact with the pool bottom. For a shallow-entry racing dive the water must be at least 0.9 m (3 ft) deep, and for a plain header dive at least 3 m (10 ft) deep. Guidance is given in the *ASA Handbook* (see **Further Reading**, page 106).
- The area for formal diving should be clearly defined and controlled. While diving is in progress, no other swimmers should be allowed in or through the area.

44 Part Three: Swimming and Diving

- Warning notices and signs should be clearly displayed, and should be regularly drawn to the attention of all pool users.
- Spacing along the pool side must be adequate to avoid the risk of collision during simultaneous dives.
- Prolonged swimming underwater after a formal dive should be discouraged.
- Raised starting blocks should be used only by experienced swimmers who are trained in their use.

Board diving Only one person should be allowed on any part of the board at any one time. The water should be checked by both the diver and the supervisor to ensure that it is clear of swimmers before a dive.

Reference should be made to pages 112–15 of the *Headteacher's Legal Guide* (see page 105).

Further reading For details of recommended reading on swimming and diving, see **Further Reading**, page 106.

Part Four
Games and Sports

Conduct and Supervision

For duty-of-care requirements for both curricular and extracurricular games and sports lessons, see **PE and the Law**, page 13.

- Before any competitive play can begin, the pupils must be given instruction in the rules of the game or sport to be pursued, as well as training in the basic skills involved.

- Training in all sports should follow a carefully planned and graduated progression, in order to ensure that the pupils have mastered the necessary skills at any given level of competence before progressing to the next stage.

- Team sizes must be restricted to the numbers approved by the relevant governing body. The length of a game should be appropriate to the age, stamina and abilities of the players.

- All games or sessions should be preceded by an adequate warm-up session.

- Jewellery and other personal effects, including watches, should be removed or securely taped before play. Sweets or gum should never be chewed.

- A routine for the safe use of the showers should be established. Temperature settings should be controllable only by the teacher. Horseplay or running through the showers is particularly dangerous.

Discipline Good conduct and a healthy attitude towards opponents should be promoted, and excessive competitiveness should be discouraged. A firm and fair interpretation of the rules, which strongly discourages bad temper, violent conduct and personal fouls, will go a long way towards eliminating dangerous play.

Clothing and equipment Clothing and equipment should always be appropriate, and should be checked before each game. Arrangements should be made for regular maintenance and repair as necessary. Faulty equipment must never be used. Pupils must know what constitutes a safe standard, and should accept responsibility for meeting that standard. Particular attention should be paid to footwear.

Equipment must be stored securely to prevent unauthorised use.

Pitches Pitches should be:

- large enough to allow safe play;
- free from dangerous objects such as stones or glass;
- level, without any depressions or bumps which might cause the ball to fly.

Special care is needed in frosty conditions, when previously muddy pitches can become dangerously ridged. Referees should be prepared to modify the game, or to postpone or cancel it if necessary. Players should be allowed to wear tracksuit bottoms on hard pitches or on synthetic surfaces, where there is a risk of skin-burn.

If a pitch has not been used for some time, or if experience shows that there is a need for frequent checks, the teacher should be ready to operate a sweep system in which both teacher and pupils scour the playing surface for hazardous debris.

Teacher participation When teachers think it appropriate to join in a game, they should consider the following points:

- Teacher participation must not reduce the effective control of the game.
- The teacher should help all pupils to become involved, and should be even-handed in the assistance provided.
- When teachers play in physical-contact games such as rugby, their natural advantages in height, weight, strength, skill and experience can easily put pupils at risk. The same applies to traditional fixtures such as staff-versus-pupils matches or those between the school and former pupils. Some national governing bodies offer guidance on this matter.

Archery

School archery should always be organised and supervised by a competent and qualified instructor. Archers should appreciate that the arrow can be a lethal weapon.

Equipment For initial teaching, bows with draw weights of 18 lb (8 kg) and 25 lb (11 kg) at 28 in (72 cm) may prove most suitable, especially for younger and smaller pupils.

Target supports should be padded to reduce the risk of rebound or ricochet. The use of drawing pins or other similar objects for attaching additional targets to the target boss should be forbidden.

Beginners should use arrows of not less than 28 in (72 cm) in length. Arrows which are too short are dangerous. At least 0.8 in (2 cm) of the arrow should be seen to project in front of the arrow rest. Arrows of 30 in (76 cm) in length may be necessary for very tall pupils, in which case at least 1.5 in (4 cm) of the arrow should be seen to project in front of the arrow rest, but not more than 5 in (12 cm).

Bracers should be worn during shooting; these keep the sleeves out of the way of the strings, and provide some measure of arm protection in the event of a bad shot. Tabs are also advisable in order to perform a clean loose and to protect the shooting fingers.

Loose clothing may foul the string and should not be worn. Neckties should be removed or tucked safely inside shirts.

Outside facilities Where there is no bank or slope behind the targets, the range should have a minimum length of 150 yd (135 m), and the targets should be positioned inside this area with at least 50 yd (45 m) clear behind them. Where there is a bank or slope of adequate height behind the target, the clear area may be reduced, but care must be taken to ensure that this area affords adequate protection to anyone moving behind the target.

The width of the range should be such that no target is positioned less than 30 yd (27 m) from public roads, rights of way or areas over which the teacher has no control.

A shooting line should be clearly marked, and a waiting line (behind which all those not actually shooting should wait) should be marked at least 5 yd (4.5 m) behind it. These lines should remain fixed, while the target should be moved as appropriate.

The whole area of the range should be clearly marked, and wherever necessary roped off.

The range should be so placed that it does not lie on the route to other playing areas. Ranges must be sited away from any buildings, walls, hedges or fences where there may be any risk of a person emerging without warning.

The grass should be cut short, and there should be no bushes or undergrowth within the range, so that stray arrows fall safely and can be easily seen.

For an illustration of the layout of an archery field according to the rules of the Grand National Archery Society, refer to the line drawing on page 16 of *Archery Today* (see **Further Reading**, page 106).

Indoor facilities The premises must be large enough for shooting at ranges of not less than 30 ft (9 m). A suitable protective device such as a fine-mesh nylon net should be provided behind the target to act as a backdrop. The effective height of this screen when in position should be at least 11 ft 6 in (3.5 m), and it should extend the full width of the hall or at least 20 ft (6 m) on either side of the target.

Entrance doors to the hall in which archery takes place should be kept locked with the key on the inside throughout the duration of the class.

Removable shutters should be provided to cover all glass panes in any doors which may be in the target area.

Organisation The number of pupils per teacher or instructor should not exceed twelve, with no more than four pupils at a target at any one time.

Targets should be at least 12 ft (3.5 m) apart, and archers should stand at least 5 ft (1.5 m) apart when they are on the shooting line.

In outdoor archery, shooting must not take place when the wind strength is such that the arrows may be dangerously deflected. Shooting directly into the wind should be avoided.

Archery should be practised only on the archery range. Bows should be loaded only on a signal from the person in charge. Archers must have their bows pointing at the target as soon as loading begins, and must be in position on the shooting line. A drawn bow, whether loaded or unloaded, should never be pointed at anyone.

Shooting should start only on a signal from the teacher or instructor.

The instructor is responsible for ensuring that the target area and the range are clear before shooting begins.

Only when all the archers have completed their shooting may the signal be given to advance to the target to retrieve the arrows. Archers should walk forward with their eyes down to detect any arrows which have fallen short.

All archers should understand the meaning of the command "fast"; when this word is shouted, they must hold onto the string and lower the bow without shooting.

All archers should understand and act instantly on the command "come down", which is used when a dangerous situation is developing. It means that the archer should hold onto the string, lower the bow, let it down to the undrawn position and remove the arrow from the bow.

When arrows are being withdrawn, the archers and others should stand at the side of the target so that there is no possibility of the withdrawer or anyone else being struck as the arrow is pulled out.

Under no circumstances should distance shooting take place. An arrow must never be shot too far upwards.

Spectators should remain at least 15 ft (4.5 m) behind the shooting line.

Association Football

Any physical-contact sport involves the risk of injury. That said, many footballing injuries can be prevented if sufficient attention is paid to playing conditions, clothing and equipment, and playing in the spirit of the game as well as to the letter.

Playing surfaces and equipment

For pitches see page 46.

Cricket stumps or stakes should not be used as improvised goals; plastic marker cones are more suitable.

For indoor five-a-side football, all movable apparatus should be cleared and unprotected lightbulbs removed. Halls with unprotected windows or low-level mirrors should never be used. Fixed apparatus near the playing area should be adequately covered (with a mat, for example).

Kit

Correct footwear is especially important: players in soft shoes risk injury to their feet. Correctly studded boots must be worn on grass. Players using synthetic pitches on a regular basis should seek advice on footwear from the national governing body (much research has been done into new types of stress injury). Modern nylon and metal studs must conform to the regulations, and should be checked regularly. Worn, sharp edges can cause serious injury. Players should carry their boots where they have to walk over hard surfaces to and from the pitch.

All players should wear shin pads.

Refereeing

In any football match a reasonable amount of robust play is inevitable. To prevent this would rob the game of much of its appeal. At the same time, the teacher in charge is responsible for the safety of the players and must be present throughout, making sure that the rules are observed (see **Discipline**, page 45).

Athletics

Responsibility for safety

Responsibility for safety lies with:

- the officials who plan the layout of facilities and organise competitions at all levels;
- the ground staff;
- teachers and coaches;
- the athletes themselves.

For insurance cover at athletics meetings, see page 30.

Facilities

The standard of facilities available should be assessed before deciding which events can be safely coached. The training area should be level, and the layout should be free of "danger zones". Throwing events must be positioned in an area set apart for the purpose.

Responsibility rests with the teacher to decide when the facilities are suitable and safe.

General safety points

The most important elements in athletics coaching are good class control, organisation and supervision. A great deal depends on the teacher–pupil relationship and the trust placed in pupils' self-discipline. Only when such trust exists should potentially dangerous events be attempted.

The most dangerous situations are likely to occur at secondary schools. Instructing a class on a school playing field is far more hazardous than coaching a select few on properly prepared facilities with full safety measures and a team of qualified helpers.

Special vigilance and control is needed when standards are being recorded (judging, measuring, time-keeping, photographing etc). Spectators should watch any competition or training from behind a barrier or at a safe distance, and should never crowd around the track or field-event areas.

When group events such as running are in progress, the teacher must remain in direct control of the group while at the same time keeping all other activities under regular supervision.

The teacher must always anticipate and allow for the mistakes of beginners and for a wide variation in standards.

Care must be taken in all events when the ground is wet. Throwing and hurdling are particularly hazardous in wet weather.

Preparation and progression in training

The teacher or coach must ensure the following:

- The athlete must be mature, fit and skilled enough to tackle each new event. The recommendations of the Schools' Athletic Association and the Schools' Consultative Committee of the Amateur Athletic Association (AAA) should be used as a guide to the events, distances etc that are suitable for primary-age pupils.

- Serious training should not begin too young, although excellent preparatory work may be possible in all events. The metabolism of children aged 9–13 works mainly aerobically, and is therefore suited to endurance-orientated activities and the learning of basic athletic skills. Specialised and technical training for "explosive" athletic activities should begin only at secondary-school age.

Field events

Field events, and especially throwing events, involve obvious hazards. They must be introduced gradually into the training programme, one event at a time, under the direct control of a qualified teacher.

The following points should be noted with regard to safe practice in field events:

Safe practice in throwing events

Much good preliminary work can be done under class instruction and by demonstration, but more detailed coaching requires smaller groups.

The coach must judge when pupils are ready to work on their own.

The routine of line-up, throwing and retrieving must be strictly enforced:

- Throwers waiting to throw should stand well behind the circle or scratch line until told to move forward. They should be well spaced and keep their eyes on the thrower in action.

- The coach must always check that the predicted line of flight, and the area around it, are clear of other pupils. A wide margin of error should be allowed for.

- Throwers must remain behind the circle or scratch line after throwing, and must never run after the implement. The implement must be retrieved only on instruction, and then carried back correctly to the circle or scratch line. It must never be thrown back.

Left-handed throwers should work together at one end of the scratch line (the thrower's left).

Where space is limited, only one pupil should be allowed to throw at a time.

Footwear must provide a firm foothold.

Implements should never be used if they are cracked or damaged in any way, and if the ground is wet they should be dried off after every throw.

Equipment should be stored securely to prevent unauthorised use.

Javelin If possible, javelins should be carried in portable storage stands which can be taken from the store onto the practice or competition area. The athlete must never run with a javelin except while throwing. When a single javelin is being moved, both ends should be covered with a block of cork or some other protective material.

Javelins should never be left stuck in the ground at a dangerous angle. At the assembly point they should be kept in a vertical position, either in the ground or in storage racks.

Before a javelin is removed from the ground, it should first be pushed up into a vertical position. It should then be carried in the same vertical position, with the point as near to the ground as possible.

Whenever possible, a surfaced area should be provided for the javelin run-up, since this gives a firmer foothold than grass.

Discus A discus with cracks, worn rims or projecting rivet heads should never be used.

Practice throwing should be confined to a safe area with adequate space for waiting throwers to stand well back.

In restricted areas, and for high-level competitions, safety nets should always be provided.

The shot Pupils should never be allowed to play with the shot, especially when other people are nearby.

Care is needed when shots are being taken from or returned to store. It is safer to carry them singly.

When competitors use rotational methods of shot-putting, they are more likely to lose control of direction and to be a danger to those in the immediate vicinity.

Hammer Hammer throwing must always be strictly controlled.

Only purpose-made hammers should be used. The spindle must be free to rotate. Bent, rusty or worn wires are dangerous.

Protective cages are essential for competition or in tightly restricted areas. The frame must be firmly fixed to the ground. The cage may be made of metal, wire mesh or fibre netting. Nylon or fibre nets must not be rigid. Guy lines must be well clear of sector lines.

Practice turns should be allowed only within the cage.

Safe practice in jumping events

General The following points should always be observed:

Sandpit landing areas Sandpit landing areas for the high jump and pole vault are safe only for low heights where the jumpers land on their feet. For more advanced training, and for competitions featuring vertical jumps, a soft landing area is required (see overleaf).

If the edges of a sandpit landing area are lined with wood or concrete, they should be flush with the ground and covered at places where a jumper is likely to hit them. A convenient and adequate cover can be made of small sacks loosely filled with cork, granular chips or rubber scrap.

The sand in the landing area should be "sharp" (non-caking) and deep enough to absorb the impact of any landing without jarring. It must be free from anything hard or sharp such as pieces of metal, wire or glass. It should be dug over after every few jumps with a fork or spade (a rake is adequate only for levelling). These implements should never be left lying near the landing area, or with the teeth pointing upwards.

Jumping must not be allowed while the landing area is being dug or raked.

Long jump and triple jump Separate runways and landing areas should be provided for long jump and triple jump. If only one of each is available, they should be wide enough for staggered boards.

Runways should be repacked and rolled when they become so worn that the edge of the take-off board is no longer level with the surface of the runway. Unless spikes are worn, grass is not a suitable take-off surface.

Take-off boards must be of regulation size, and must be firmly fixed to the runway: a loose board can cause serious injury to the instep. They should be painted in a distinguishing colour and kept clean and dry.

If there is only one take-off board for the triple jump, its position may be either too near the landing area for senior pupils or too far away for juniors. So several boards should be used, and should be placed at distances of 7 m, 9 m, 11 m and 13 m from the landing area.

High jump and pole vault In the high jump, the athlete must be taught that the take-off position largely determines the landing position.

Round bars are recommended, especially for "flop" styles of jumping. When "flexi-bars" are used, the supporting stands must be secured so as not to collapse onto the jumper.

Soft landing areas Soft, multi-unit landing areas are essential when jumpers use styles which involve landing on the back and upper part of the neck. These should conform to the following requirements:

Size In high-jump training, where the take-off point can be satisfactorily dictated by the coach, a unit size of 4 m x 2.5 m (13 ft x 8 ft) is needed.

In competitions the landing area must be large enough to allow safe use by all competitors, irrespective of jumping style. The area should conform to the sizes recommended by the AAA for the level and age range of the competition.

Cushioning material Cushioning material must be deep and dense enough to prevent "bottoming out" — that is, any landing must be completely absorbed. Suppliers should be asked to provide relevant data on bottoming out. Reference tables to check this are available from responsible mat manufacturers and from the British Amateur Athletics Board.

Landing surface Landing surfaces must be all-weather, low-friction and resistant to wear from spikes and trainers. Units should also be closely linked by adequate tying points to give an even cushioning effect.

> Details of the dimensions of soft landing areas are given on pages 34–5 of *Facilities for Athletics — Track and Field*, and also in the AAA Rules for Competition (see **Further Reading**, pages 106–7).

Soft landing areas deteriorate over time, and need regular inspection, with appropriate maintenance and repair throughout the season.

Some responsibility rests with the athletes in these events to check that the landing area is safe and suitable.

Poles and take-off boxes Fibre poles can soften and snap after extensive use. They should be examined regularly, and discarded if they are cracked or spiked. They should always be treated with care, and kept in a box when not in use.

Fibre poles should never be used in planting boxes which have a vertical backplate, as these do not allow the pole to achieve its full bend.

Field events in competition
Athletes should always be suitably prepared, and should have reached the qualifying standard for the competition.

The regulations and recommendations of the association under whose rules the competition is being run should be carefully studied and followed.

> **From the AAA Rules for Competition:**
>
> **1** Throwing sectors should be roped off to avoid accidents. The ropes should be well away from the sector lines marked on the ground for each event.
>
> **2** Instructions should be given that, during both practice and competition, implements must be thrown only from the circles or scratch lines or their immediate vicinity. Implements must be returned by hand, never thrown back to the starting area.
>
> **3** Prominent notices should be displayed outside the ropes to warn any spectators who may unthinkingly step over or under the ropes.
>
> **4** Circle and scratch lines must be sited so as to avoid the possibility of the implement landing among the spectators, or among judges or competitors in other events, either in a fair throw or if an implement slips from the competitor's hand.
>
> **5** Definite instructions must be given as to whether the competitor or the steward is to retrieve and return the implement.
>
> **6** One of the judges should stand in the circle, on the scratch line or in front of the take-off board while a throw or jump is being measured, to make sure that the next competitor does not make his or her attempt until all is clear.
>
> **7** A loud-hailer or some other form of audible warning is of great assistance to the judges of field events.

Track events

- Great self-discipline and control are necessary to prevent accidents and injury from spikes. Instructions on their safe use should be given at the earliest opportunity.

- When spikes are worn, numbers in events should be strictly limited. In the 800-metres, for example, there should be a maximum of eight athletes.

- All races of one lap or less should be run in lanes. Observance of this rule is particularly important at the changeover in relay races.

- In races of more than one lap, the start should be organised so that the runners are well spaced, and the number of runners should be limited to avoid bunching or collision early on.

- Finishing tapes should be made from a length of worsted which breaks easily. They should be positioned no higher than chest-height.

- Hurdles should be rigidly constructed with a smooth rounded finish, free from sharp or protruding edges. They must be of the correct weight and resistance as detailed in the AAA's rule book. The legs and feet must be set at right angles to the top-bar.

- Starting blocks, hammers, nails and other material should be removed from the track immediately after use.

- For advice on starting pistols, see below.

Cross-country

- The start should be sufficiently wide to accommodate the number of runners safely.

- There should be a long, clear approach run to allow the competitors to sort themselves out before the first obstacle. This obstacle should be sufficiently wide to prevent bunching up or queueing.

- First aid and casualty transport should be provided at various points *en route*, and the base facilities should include hot drinks and showers, washing and changing facilities.

- On all runs, pupils should be counted at the start, *en route* and at the finish. Short cuts should be strictly forbidden.

- Courses must be graded for different abilities. The slowest runner should be tailed throughout the race so that runners who are injured or in distress can be located and escorted back for treatment.

- All runners should take a hot shower afterwards.

Starting pistols There is no such thing as a safe firearm. Large-bore starting pistols, and those capable of conversion to take live ammunition, are all subject to licence, regular police notification and strict safety precautions. Even loose ammunition, or the small-calibre gun normally used in schools, can be dangerous in inexperienced hands.

A starting pistol should always be fired at arm's length above the head.

The pistol should never be left loaded. After use the slide or magazine should be removed, the ammunition extracted, and the gun, slide and ammunition locked away in a safe place.

For security reasons all starting pistols should be marked with the name of the owner or school. The loss of guns or ammunition should be reported immediately.

When .38 blank ammunition is used, the starter should wear earmuffs.

Basketball

Rules Basketball is played at speed, in a confined space, on a hard surface and usually on a court surrounded by obstacles. It must be played as a non-contact sport from the learning stages onwards.

Footwear Specially designed basketball boots are desirable. Players should never play in bare or stockinged feet.

Court The court surface should be clean, dry and non-slip. Any protruding obstruction closer than one metre (40 in) to the side- or end-lines should be removed or padded, especially if it is behind the line of the backboards.

Equipment There is a British Standard specification for basketball and mini-basketball equipment (BS 1892 Section 2.7). The English Basketball Association recommends that, wherever possible, posts and boards for use out of doors should be permanently fixed into the ground.

Backboards Where possible these should have an overhang of 125 cm (50 in) on match courts and 75 cm (30 in) on practice courts. Backboards should normally be fitted by specialist contractors.

Rings and baskets Regulation-pattern rings and baskets should be used, and not rings with hooks or spring clips for the attachment of baskets. The basket should be no longer than 40 cm (16 in), with fine nylon mesh.

Balls These should not be over-inflated, and should be inspected regularly for splits or other damage.

Boxing

The PE profession has always been concerned to minimise the risk of accidents and injury to pupils.

It is now recognised that blows to the head, if delivered with force and frequency, can cause damage to the brain and also to the eyes, ears and mouth.

BAALPE's view is that, since the risk of injury cannot be avoided in boxing, schools would be unwise to include boxing as part of their PE curriculum.

Cricket

Cricket played recreationally with a soft ball presents no special risk. But when it is played as a team game with a hard leather ball, the following points should be considered:

Dress and equipment Studded boots or shoes provide a firmer foothold for all players. Batters should wear batting gloves, pads, abdominal guards and (for boys) a box. The wicket-keeper should wear the same protective equipment, but with wicket-keeping gloves instead of batting gloves.

Bats and protective gear should be matched in size, weight and design to the age, strength and ability of the players.

Facilities The playing surface should be true. A bumpy or uneven surface is unsafe for both batters and fielders. Pitches should be provided with a reasonable boundary — 50 m (55 yd), for example — and sited to avoid the risk of balls being hit onto paths or roadways, or into private property or public areas.

Artificial wickets If a grass wicket is not available, a suitable artificial wicket should be used. This should be kept in good repair, and matting surfaces should be securely fastened so that the whole length gives a true surface.

Net practice Protective netting should be provided in coaching areas, and should be so arranged as to give protection to players in adjoining bays. It should be inspected frequently and kept in good repair.

Bowlers at net practice should be sure that their fielders and batters are alert and ready to play. The bowler should call "play" before bowling the first ball, and then at any time after that when it seems necessary.

Balls should not be collected from inside the net while play is in progress. Non-participants, including players waiting their turn to bat, should remain behind the nets.

Safe play Play should not begin until the umpire at the bowler's end is sure that all players are concentrating on the game and ready to start. The umpire should call "play" before the first ball is bowled.

Fielders should not stand too near the bat, especially on the leg side.

The English Schools Cricket Association's rule restricting the placing of fielders states that:

> *No fielder in under-14 or under-15 cricket games, except the wicket-keeper, shall be allowed to field nearer than eight yards, measured from the middle stump, except behind the wicket on the off-side. A fielder shall be allowed to move into the restricted area to make a catch or field a ball provided that he [or she] was outside the area when the stroke was made. At the under-13 level and below, the distance shall be 11 yards.*

- Where it proves helpful, umpires should have a mark laid down to assist in determining the distance.
- Umpires should hold up play if a fielder is within the restricted distance.

Cycling

General The Cycling Teaching Certificate is a basic qualification designed to enable all concerned to introduce cycling into the normal PE programme or as an extracurricular activity.

All cycling activities should be approved by the headteacher and parents.

Bicycle safety All cycles should be checked for safety and suitability (see also the ROSPA *Cycle Safety* leaflets, listed in **Further Reading**, page 107).

- The saddle height should be adjusted so that the rider can sit comfortably on the saddle with one foot on the ground.
- Both front and rear brakes must be efficient, with conveniently placed brake levers.
- The tyres and lights should meet all current standards and regulations before a module of work can begin. The local police will need to make frequent checks, and excellent cooperation can be expected.

Group riding Group discipline is essential for cycling on the road:

- Groups should be small: seven is the recommended number for one adult leader.

- Group riding should first be practised on the school playground or in a similar off-road location.
- The group leader should ride at the back of the group on the outside, so that the whole group can be observed and instructions can be called out as necessary.
- The leader should appoint two reliable riders to be the leading pair, and should instruct them clearly to maintain a steady pace.
- There should always be a minimum of one bicycle-length between riders. When cyclists are riding in pairs, they should avoid riding too close together.
- Riders should always warn those behind of any obstacles or hazards ahead, such as potholes or parked cars, either by giving the correct hand signals or by calling out.
- Riders should glance behind occasionally to ensure that those following have not fallen too far behind.
- All sudden actions such as stopping without warning should be avoided.
- On narrow and twisting roads, and in heavy or fast-moving traffic, single file should be maintained, with a minimum of one bicycle-length between riders.

Moving into single file This can be learned by using the following routine, which should first be mastered off the road:

- The group leader lines the riders up in pairs a safe distance apart, and instructs them to ride round at a steady pace.
- At the order to move into single file, each inside rider slips carefully into place behind the outside rider.
- The leader can then hold back the traffic if necessary, give the order to continue single-file riding, and wave traffic on when it is safe to do so and the group is all in single file.

Races Races should be organised only by experienced or qualified officials who meet the requirements of the appropriate national governing bodies. Separate rules govern the different types of racing, and many of these rules deal with safety. The English Schools Cycling Association supplies advice sheets on the organisation of cyclo-cross, time trials, circuit and track racing (see **Further Reading**, page 107).

Fencing

General Teachers should set a good example at all times: they should never fence without a mask, or give lessons dressed casually in a tracksuit top.

At no time should inexperienced pupils be allowed to fence without qualified supervision and the correct equipment. Although "free play" should be encouraged at the earliest opportunity, supervision is necessary to prevent wild, uncontrolled movements.

Clothing and equipment

One-hundred-per-cent protection is impossible in fencing, but the risk of injury can be greatly reduced if the correct clothing is worn and the right equipment is used.

Fencers should never cross swords unless wearing full protective clothing, consisting of mask, plastron, jacket and gloves.

Mask

The mask should be sound, and complete with bib. Masks must not be worn if the mesh shows signs of rust, displaced wire or undue denting. The binding around the mesh should be in good repair, and the bib which protects the throat should be sound and strongly sewn to the mask. The mask must fit properly, with an effective head clip.

Jacket

Jackets must be of the right size and of the type approved by the Amateur Fencing Association's Schools' Fencing Union. They should also be kept in good repair: a broken blade could result in the tip of the sword catching a small hole. Where jackets have side fastenings, right-handed fencers must wear right-handed jackets with the opening on the left-hand side — and vice versa. Jackets should be long enough to cover the waistband of the trousers (the official requirement is a 10-cm (4-in) overlap when in the *en garde* position).

At epée it is particularly important not to use a lightweight zip jacket. An epée jacket should be used, and it should be made of material weighing at least 400 g/m^2 (12 oz/sq yd).

The recently introduced training jacket with one-arm coverage must not be used in competition.

Plastron

A plastron must be worn for all fencing practice and competitions. A simple tee-shirt under the jacket is not enough.

Breeches

Fencing breeches are a requirement for competitions. The side opening should correspond to that of the jacket — that is, on the opposite side to that of the sword arm. Long white socks should be worn to cover the legs below the breeches.

Gloves

Gloves should have a gauntlet to cover the cuff of the jacket sleeve, protecting the wrist and arm. The gauntlet must extend halfway up the forearm to ensure a safe overlap.

Weapons

> Fencing must stop if any item of equipment becomes damaged.

Weapons must be regularly checked. Swords with broken, badly bent or rusting blades must never be used. Any blades which bend and stay bent show weakness and should be condemned. Much-used weapons can be dangerous, developing very sharp edges around the guard circumference, which can cause quite severe cuts on an opponent's knee, leg or hand. Points should be covered with purpose-made protective tips.

Floors Floors should be checked before use. Injuries may result from fencing on highly polished or dusty floors, both of which may be slippery.

Control of space in competition There should be a distance of at least 1.5 m (5 ft) between pistes, and a clear run-off area at both ends of each piste for the safety of competitors and spectators.

Spectators should sit or stand well away from the fencing; it is impossible to give a precise distance, as this will depend on the standard and level of the fencing.

Emergencies A first-aid kit should always be available, together with the address and telephone number of the nearest doctor and hospital.

Gaelic Sports

The Department of Education for Northern Ireland (DENI) endorses the Gaelic Athletic Association's specific recommendations on personal protective clothing (see page 112 for contact point).

Golf

Indoor lessons Airflow plastic balls should be used unless a good net is provided.

If hard golf balls are used, the following points are important:

- A special golf net with a fine mesh should be used; it should be at least 2.5 m (8 ft) high and should hang clear of any supports.

- Suitable protective mats should always be used on the floor. This also applies when airflow practice balls are used.

- Players should be at least 3 m (10 ft) apart at all times when handling clubs. During demonstrations this distance should be maintained between the demonstrator and the nearest pupil.

- Players driving at a net should remain strictly in line.

- No player should advance to collect balls or for any other purpose until all the balls have been struck by the other players. Balls should be retrieved only on a given signal.

- If players are using both sides of the net at the same time, only airflow balls should be used. The mesh should be examined regularly for damage.

- Players should not walk up to one another during practice to discuss technique.

Outdoor lessons The following layouts are acceptable, whether for practising strokes or for playing shots:

- a straight line of players facing in one direction;

- two straight lines at least 6 m (20 ft) apart and facing away from each other;

- a semicircle facing outwards.

The distance between players should be not less than 3 m (10 ft).

> No player should play a shot of any kind if anyone is in the line of flight and might conceivably be hit.

When players are practising in a straight line, no player should be in advance of any other.

No player should advance into the target area until all the balls have been hit. All balls should be collected at the same time on a given signal.

No player should practise out of a sand bunker if any other player is near the line of flight.

Play on golf courses All players should learn the rules of golf, and beginners in particular should gain a thorough knowledge of the section on etiquette.

Hockey

Hockey, like other physical-contact games, contains an element of danger, but good coaching and facilities, firm control and care of equipment can reduce this to a minimum.

Facilities For general safety of pitches, see page 46. Grass pitches should be cut and rolled regularly to ensure that the ball runs true.

Goals should be kept in good order and regularly painted. Portable goals should be secured to prevent them from tipping over.

Corner flags should be a minimum of 4 ft (1.2 m) and a maximum of 5 ft (1.5 m) high. The top of the post must not be pointed.

Control of the game The rules of hockey go into considerable detail. In coaching, particular emphasis should be placed on those rules concerning dangerous play, the use of the stick, body interference and obstruction.

The umpire should keep firm control, but should allow play to continue wherever possible. Bad temper, dangerous play and personal fouls should be penalised. Umpiring at school level always involves an element of education.

Good coaching will lead to good habits. Practising skills will help players to get a feel for the stick and the ball, and will reduce the chance of dangerous play.

Goalkeepers should be discouraged from using the lying-down technique to defend penalty corners. Only the traditional methods of goalkeeping should be taught.

Equipment and clothing The footwear should be appropriate to the particular playing surface, and should be regularly checked for safety. Poor footwear used regularly on artificial pitches may cause stress to the lower back, knees and ankles.

Players should wear mouthguards and shin pads. When playing on artificial pitches, they should be allowed to wear tracksuit trousers because of the risk of skin-burn.

Goalkeepers must always be well protected and equipped. They should wear adequate pads and kickers, gauntlet gloves, abdominal protection and a full helmet and mask.

Sticks must be kept in good condition, and must never be allowed to become dangerous through roughness, splinters or other faults.

Horse-riding

Qualifications The minimum qualification for the teaching of horse-riding is the Assistant Instructor's Certificate of the British Horse Society.

Safety Horse-riding should take place only at a riding establishment approved by the British Horse Society.

Teachers should enforce the specific safety precautions drawn up by the riding establishment.

Parental permission should always be obtained before a course of lessons begins.

All riders should wear appropriate protective headgear which meets the current BSI standard, and shoes with sharply defined heels which will not slide forward through the stirrup.

Judo

Competence to teach

The judo grade, shown by the colour of the belt, indicates the level of proficiency in the sport, but does not measure teaching ability. The various national judo organisations in the UK have different requirements for their teaching certificates.

The minimum requirement for a person with qualified-teacher status to teach judo in a school is either the green belt (British Judo Association 5th kyu) or the British Judo Association's Teacher Certificate. A visiting coach (ie a person without qualified-teacher status) should have been awarded at least a brown belt (1st kyu), and should also have completed a course in the teaching or coaching of the sport.

The minimum qualification for an instructor in further education (including the youth service) is a brown belt (1st kyu), together with the completion of a recognised course in the teaching or coaching of the sport.

Mats

There is a range of mats specifically designed for judo.

Mats must be dense and firm enough to minimise the risk of injury. The density of any mat can be tested by striking it sharply with the elbow to see if it "bottoms". There should be sufficient firmness to avoid excessive sinking and drag during movement about the mat. If the floor below has no resilience (if it is made of concrete, for example), then the thickness of the mat may need to be increased.

The individual mats making up a judo area must be secured in position and not allowed to separate. A canvas cover should not be used; neither should a bulky and potentially dangerous "frame" to hold the mats together.

The mat area should measure a minimum of 5.5 m x 5.5 m (approximately 18 ft x 18 ft) or 7 m x 5 m (approximately 23 ft x 16 ft). Unless the mat area is exceptionally large, no edge should be within 2 m (6 ft) of any wall, projection or open door. There should be a ceiling height of at least 3 m (10 ft).

Clothing

Participants must wear judo jackets, trousers and belts. Judo suits should be hygienically stored and regularly laundered.

Class organisation

The number of participants should be limited according to the area of mat available. In free practice (randori) it is reasonable to permit 11 sq m (approximately 10 ft x 10 ft) for each competing pair, but this area can be increased for formal class teaching, when there may be fewer people on the mats. These figures may need to be varied according to the size of the participants.

No pair should practise throwing techniques while other pairs are practising groundwork techniques.

Both sexes can be taught together in judo. However, boys' judo is physically stronger than girls', and uses some different techniques. There should never be any form of contest between the sexes.

Lacrosse

Men's lacrosse

Protective clothing Men's lacrosse is a fast-moving contact sport. The amount of protective clothing needed at senior level depends on the standard of the game.

Gauntlets should always be worn, and should be well padded on the outside of the hand and wrist. A rigid or padded cap is desirable to protect the head and face; it should be fitted with a mask and chinstrap, and properly fastened on both sides.

The goalkeeper should wear chest, stomach and thigh pads and an abdominal protector.

In international lacrosse the wearing of all this protection is mandatory. At junior level such equipment is not compulsory, but all players are advised to wear as much of it as possible.

Pop lacrosse Pop lacrosse is the ideal introduction to the game. It incorporates the basic skills and strategies of the field game, but has more flexible rules, which can be adapted to suit the players involved, their equipment and the playing area. There is no stick or body contact.

Women's lacrosse

Women's lacrosse is a non-contact sport. The rules are specifically designed to protect players, especially around the head.

Players should wear gloves. These must be close-fitting, with no webbing or excessive padding. Boots with metal studs must not be worn.

More and more players, particularly at international level, choose to wear gum shields. Other protection such as nose guards may be worn, but field players are not allowed to wear protective headgear or face masks.

Goalkeepers should wear leg pads, a body pad and a face mask and/or helmet.

Martial Arts

Aikido

Competence to teach — Only instructors qualified as Martial Arts Commission (MAC) coaches should teach aikido, either within or outside the curriculum. They must have a current MAC licence and instructor's indemnity insurance, which complements the third-party liability cover in force within LEA or school-owned premises.

Clothing and equipment — A loose-fitting tunic is essential, and the correct trousers are preferable. Mats should fulfil the requirements laid down for judo (see page 65). Further information is given in the MAC *Guidelines* (see **Further Reading**, page 107).

Class organisation — Aikido can be conducted as a mixed activity except in competition. Where older pupils are practising regularly, they should take out an MAC licence.

A qualified instructor will ensure that no dangerous locks or movements will either be taught or practised.

Karate

Karate classes mainly practise kihon (basic technique: single kicking or punching sequences) and kata (stylised, controlled, predetermined movements).

Competence to teach — Only instructors qualified as Martial Arts Commission (MAC) or British Karate Control Commission (BKCC) coaches should be allowed to teach karate within or outside the curriculum. They should have a current licence and indemnity insurance to complement the third-party liability cover in force within LEA or school-owned premises.

All licences should bear the heading Martial Arts Commission or British Karate Control Commission.

There are various styles of karate. An instructor's style is acceptable if he or she has been graded by an association or organisation that is a member of the English, Scottish or Welsh Karate Board. There are few national awards or courses organised specifically for the teaching or coaching of the sport, so the grade of the applicant is the only criterion of assessment.

The minimum requirement for a person with qualified-teacher status to teach karate in schools is 3rd kyu. A visiting coach (ie a person without qualified-teacher status) should have at least 1st kyu. An instructor in further education (including the youth service) should hold at least 1st kyu.

Clothing A karate jacket is essential, and the correct trousers are preferable. Clothing should be stored hygienically and laundered regularly.

Class organisation Free fighting (jy-yu-kumite) should take place only under the instructor's direct control. He or she should authorise it only when satisfied that the participants have sufficient mastery of the techniques of attack and defence.

Each individual requires 3 sq m (11 sq ft) of space for basic technique and 4 sq m (19 sq ft) for kata.

Supplementary weapons should not be permitted.

An instructor should use only minimum force when correcting a student's position or movement.

Karate classes can include both sexes, but free fighting between boys and girls is not acceptable.

Recommended reading See **Further Reading**, page 107.

Kendo

Competence to teach The British Kendo Association (BKA) is the national governing body for the sport. It provides training and awards certificates at various levels. The minimum grade for teaching kendo in schools, further education and the youth service is 1st dan.

Equipment The wearing of armour (mask, body padding and gauntlets) is essential for free fighting. This should be stored where it can dry naturally and hygienically. The shinai (dummy sword) should be of the traditional type; it should be maintained in good condition and checked regularly.

Class organisation In kata practice only wooden swords (bokuto) should be used.

Iaido is a type of kendo that uses bokker (bokuto), iaito (specially blunted swords) for iaido practice, or real swords. Iaido should only be practised under BKA-approved instructors who also have the 1st dan grade in iaido. The minimum qualification required is the BKA/MAC Assistant Coach Award.

In iaido practice, only iaito should normally be used.

In both kata and iaido, permission should be obtained from the BKA before real swords can be used for any demonstration or practice. Permission will be given only to advanced performers.

Other martial arts

There are numerous other martial arts that can be described as variations of karate. Some require the use of weapons, while others permit full bodily contact when striking or kicking. Both types can be hazardous. Advice should be sought from the MAC when considering the suitability of any of these other martial arts for classes.

Netball

Netball is a non-contact game. The official rules of the All England Netball Association (AENA), which prohibit physical contact and rough play, should be enforced.

A simplified version of the official netball rules for those working with players under the age of eleven is also available from the AENA.

Court The court surface should be firm, level and non-slip. There should be a minimum of 1 m (3 ft 3 in) of space between the outside lines of the court and any netting, wall, kerb edging or other obstruction. There should be a minimum of 2 m (6 ft 7 in) of space between adjacent courts.

Indoor courts should be free of furniture or other obstructions.

Post and rings These should comply with AENA rules. The posts should be stable; if they are free-standing, the bases should be of metal and weighted as necessary to ensure stability. The bases should not project into the court area, and should be checked regularly for rust.

Clothing and hygiene Fingernails should be short, and clothing should allow the player sufficient freedom to run and jump with safety.

Gloves may be worn only if they are needed for medical reasons, and then only on production of an appropriate medical certificate. The umpires must be satisfied that the gloves do not present a hazard to other players.

Further Reading See **Further Reading**, page 107.

Racket Games

All these games (tennis, squash, badminton and fives) are comparatively safe, although recent research has revealed a high incidence of eye injuries.

Accidents may arise from:

- players being struck by a racket
- players being struck by a ball or shuttlecock

- players tripping or slipping
- players wearing unsuitable or damaged footwear.

Equipment In tennis, sponge or "short tennis" balls are recommended for use in crowded areas.

In squash, players should wear protective eye shields.

Playing areas Lines on courts should be flat, level and securely fixed.

Shale or similar non-grass courts should be watered and rolled regularly to ensure a firm, level surface.

When courts have been made slippery by rain, then play or practice must be delayed until the surface has dried out.

Nets and surrounding netting should be kept in good order.

Netball and basketball posts should not be left on the playing area.

Organisation Class numbers and the positioning of players need careful planning.

When players are practising serving, smashing or lobbing, a routine drill is needed to prevent accidents. In service practice there should be a maximum of six players behind the baseline. In particular, feeders should never be placed directly in front of players practising the smash. Players waiting their turn should be outside the court and well spaced, so that if necessary they can move quickly to avoid being hit.

Sufficient space must be allowed for the stroke that is being played, including an allowance for any follow-through.

Group formations should be designed so as to ensure that players moving backwards cannot collide with other players or with a wall or fencing.

In tennis or badminton, three groups of two can be safely accommodated on one court in rallying situations: one group within each set of tramlines, and a third group in the middle of the court.

Players should never:

- try to play shots outside their own playing area;
- go onto other courts to retrieve balls or shuttlecocks while play is in progress;
- look round at a partner who is serving;
- jump over or duck under the net when changing ends;

- leave balls, rackets, shuttlecocks etc lying on the court.

In squash, a player intentionally impeding an opponent should be penalised for the offence of interference.

Rounders

In rounders the striker should always carry the stick when running. It can be dangerous to throw away the stick before reaching first base.

Rowing

The teaching of rivercraft should take priority over the teaching of rowing skills. Before pupils even enter a boat, they should be told about the local navigation rules, and about the nature and effect of currents, weirs, sluices, bridges and winds. The rights and customs of other users of the waterways should also be covered.

The parents' written consent should be obtained before a pupil takes part in rowing.

Equipment Craft should be inspected both before and after a rowing session for leaks and faulty fittings.

The coaching launch should carry the following items:

- a bailer
- a klaxon or warning device which is audible over 200 m (650 ft)
- a grab line
- lifebuoys
- safety devices for normal use in a launch.

Clothing Coxswains should wear lifejackets, and clothing suited to the weather conditions, but never wellingtons or heavy footwear.

Before launch
- No pupil should be allowed on the water unless he or she can swim 50 m (165 ft) in light clothing.
- All crews should be instructed in procedures in the event of a capsize or other type of accident while rowing. Capsize drill should preferably be practised under safe conditions.
- No crew should launch unless the teacher or instructor has decided that conditions are suitable.

On the water
- Coaching launches should not act as pacers.

- Teachers or coaches should normally keep all their craft within view. Only an experienced crew or sculler should be allowed to row out of sight, and then only on a prescribed course.

- In the event of fog, all crews should return to their boathouses.

After dark Normally there should be no rowing after dusk. If rowing after dark is the custom, boats must be equipped with a headlight or navigation lights as locally required, and the coxswain should have a waterproof torch with a strong beam. The accompanying launch should carry navigation lights and spare torches.

Further information See **Further Reading**, page 107.

Rugby Union and Rugby League

The strenuous physical-contact nature of rugby means that safety must be given paramount importance.

Direct supervision by teachers with a good knowledge of the game is required. Refereeing should be firm.

Clothing and personal protection

- Boots should be firm-fitting with ankle support.

- Studs should conform to BS 6366, and should be examined regularly for wear. Badly worn studs can be very dangerous for the wearer and for the other players.

- Shin guards should be worn by all forwards. They should be made of a light material and strapped on.

- Shoulder pads (for Rugby League only) should consist of no more than light, flexible protective padding.

- Mouth guards are a valuable means of protection, but great care must be taken to make sure they fit correctly. (Details can be found in the Rugby Football Union's *Player Improvement Plan*; see **Further Reading**, page 107.)

Facilities and equipment For general safety of pitches, see page 46.

- There should be no dangerous obstructions close to the perimeter of the field. Fertilisers and mixtures used for pitch marking should be free from irritants, particularly lime or creosote.

- The bases of the uprights of the goalposts should be padded.

- Corner flags should be flexible.

Coaching The teaching of good technique in skills such as those for tackling, scrummaging and falling on the ball will not only improve playing standards but will also make the game safer. Players must be taught the fundamental skills before they play competitively.[1]

The pupil–teacher ratio should never be higher than 30 to one, and opposing teams should be comparable in age and physique.

First aid An adequate kit should be available. Knowledge of basic first aid and expired-air resuscitation (see page 31) should be sufficient to deal with immediate injuries.

Further information See **Further Reading**, page 107.

Skating

Skating, whether on ice or on rollers, is often taught by a professional skater who is employed at a rink. That said, teachers should supervise throughout the session, with special vigilance during periods of free practice.

Rules drawn up by individual rink managers must be strictly observed.

Ice-skating

Clothing Clothing should be suitable, and should include protection for the legs. Gloves should be worn by beginners.

Care should be taken to select the correct size of boot.

On the rink
- All skating should be in an anticlockwise direction.
- No more than two people should be allowed to skate linked together.
- The centre of the rink should be left free for figure-skaters.
- Speed-skating should be severely restricted.

Roller-skating

Skating should not begin until the floor has been checked.

Clothing and equipment Clothing should be suitable, and should include protection for the legs. Ties, jackets and scarves should be removed before skating.

Strong walking shoes should be worn, so that skates can be fitted correctly.

---

1 Particular note should be taken of the differing results of two recent court cases in connection with incidents at Bedford Modern School and Exeter College.

Pockets should be emptied of bulky articles, and long hair should be tied back.

On the rink
- All skating should be in an anticlockwise direction unless the coach directs otherwise.
- No more than three people should be allowed to skate linked together.
- Chasing games should not be allowed.
- Speed-skating should be severely restricted.

Trampolining

Trampolining is an established part of PE in many secondary schools, and is taught outside the curriculum in some middle and primary schools. It offers an exciting challenge to the more able child, and when carefully controlled it can stimulate movement in disabled or mentally handicapped pupils. Both trampolines and trampettes can, however, produce serious accidents. Each LEA or EA formulates its own regulations on the use of these rebound surfaces.

The following recommendations are made:

The teacher For advanced trampolining, teachers or coaches should hold the appropriate award of the British Trampoline Federation. A special award for teachers of children with SEN is currently in preparation.

Class organisation The trampoline should be under the teacher's or coach's direct supervision, and should be positioned so as to minimise the risk of children being distracted.

An experienced teacher should be able to supervise several trampolines at once. This requires:

- a good all-round viewing position that allows the teacher to instruct pupils on any trampoline;
- individual routines approved by the teacher;
- competent spotting.

The pupils
- Pupils should mount the trampoline by stepping onto the frame and then the bed, not onto the springs or cables. Dismounting should follow the reverse procedure. No one should jump from the trampoline bed directly onto the floor.
- Pupils should jump from as near to the centre of the bed as possible, and should bounce up no further than the maximum height at which they retain complete control.

- Beginners should bounce only for short periods such as 30 seconds. The jumping time can then be extended, but should stop as soon as the pupil starts to tire or lose concentration.

- The basic bounces must be mastered separately before sequences and more advanced skills are attempted. Individual check-off charts will help to record progress.

- Only one pupil should be allowed on the trampoline at any one time, except in advanced work.

- "Tag-on" games, in which one performer adds a movement to the routine of those going before, are not recommended; they may induce a performer to work beyond his or her ability.

- In competitions and displays, only those movements that have been successfully consolidated in practice should be performed. No one should attempt new records, such as in the number of repetitions of a given movement.

High-flight rotational skills These can be dangerous, and novices should never be asked to attempt them. The same applies to forward rolls on landing: inexperienced pupils should be trained instead to make a controlled landing on two feet.

The trampoline
- Solid beds are appropriate for performers of very limited ability.

- Trampolines, especially those with steel springs, should be equipped with frame pads. The "coverall" type removes the risk of landing directly on the metal frame or falling through the gaps between the springs or cables.

- Springs or cables must be swapped around frequently (ie the centre ones should be transferred towards the corners of the frame and vice versa) so as to minimise loss of tension. When a small number of new springs is fitted, then these should be spaced out.

Functional check When the trampoline has been assembled, check the following points:

- That all leg braces have been properly fitted and that the hinge units are securely housed.

- That all adjustments are tight.

- That the hooks of the springs are properly attached, with the ends pointing downwards.

- That the cables are in good condition.

- That the springs on "learner" trampolines are made of rubber rather than steel.

- That the safety pads are in place.

- That if allen screws are present these are tight.

- That the bed is clean.
- That the wheeling devices are operating smoothly, and that the pivotal housing on the frame holds the hub of the wheeling mechanism at right angles, without any movement between the hub and the housing.
- That the wheel units have been removed to a storage position well clear of the trampoline area.

Positioning

- Check that the trampoline is placed well away from any overhead obstructions (hanging beams, lights etc); there should be an overhead clearance of at least 5 m (16 ft) from the floor to the lowest hanging object (some trampolines may require even greater clearance).
- Check that the space is clear immediately around and beneath the trampoline.

Unfolding and folding the trampoline

Pupils should be taught how to unfold and fold the trampoline under direct supervision. They should never pull the trampoline towards them or walk underneath it.

Unfolding Ensure that:

- The wheels are kept well away from people's feet.
- The trampoline is angled and lowered carefully, and the lower leg section is held firmly so that it does not crash to the floor.
- The frame sections are opened with a firm, continuous movement to prevent them springing back.
- Fingers, elbows and wrists are kept clear of all the hinges.

Folding Ensure that:

- The wheels are securely housed.
- The frame sections are closed using a firm, continuous, controlled movement, resisting the tension in the springs or cables.
- Fingers, elbows and wrists are kept clear of all the hinges.
- People's feet are kept well away from the wheels.
- The lower frame and leg sections are positioned inside the upper frame and leg sections as the trampoline is rotated from the horizontal to the vertical.

When folded, the trampoline should be locked to prevent unauthorised use; this can be done simply by locking together two of the links in one of the leg chains.

Spotters There should always be a minimum of four and a maximum of six spotters, who should be spaced out around the trampoline. They must know exactly what their role is, and should be physically capable of performing their tasks. They must also be given clear instructions.

Supporting aids Overhead rigs, crash mats, support harnesses and manual support are all recognised aids for the coaching of advanced trampolining. Crash mattresses should be placed at each end of the trampoline, and another should be available to be thrown between the performer and the bed during the learning of new movements or if a poor landing seems likely. Multi-somersaulting and twisting movements should be learned in an overhead support rig.

Bed-level platforms should be used by coaches for supervision, and so that they can intervene when necessary.

Trampette activities

Functional check All adjustment nuts must be tight.

Use of the trampette for beginners
- The trampette should not be used as part of any apparatus sequence until adequate training has first been given in the basic techniques of jumping and landing from it.
- Beginners should start with slow, controlled practice runs of not more than five paces.

Using the trampette at more advanced levels
- Each stage should be consolidated before progressing to the next.
- Support should be appropriate to the skill being practised. Support may be provided by trained pupils if the class is working well. The supporter should check pupils as they land, and should be able to prevent them from falling backwards or pitching forwards.

High-flight rotational skills These can be dangerous, and novices should never be asked to attempt them. The same applies to forward rolls on landings: inexperienced pupils should be trained instead to make a controlled landing on two feet.

Teaching somersaults The teacher must provide appropriate support at every stage, especially with older or heavier pupils.

The teacher must beware of overthrow. This is most often caused by:

- pupils maintaining a position such as the pike or the tuck for too long during flight;
- too tight a tuck position in the early stages and holding the position for too long.

Beginners should concentrate first on perfecting a good take-off technique. When there is the slightest suspicion of overthrow, the teacher or supporters must stand by ready to check and steady the landing.

Beginners must never perform a forward roll immediately after the front somersault, as to do this safely requires considerable control and understanding. They should always land in a standing position, with the coach standing by.

The supporter must do everything possible to prevent the performer from landing on the head or neck.

Learners should not attempt unsupported somersaults until they have demonstrated complete confidence and mastery. Even then, someone should stand by during the first session.

> **NB** Leaping over a distance to swing on a gymnastic beam is dangerous and should not be allowed.

Volleyball

Facilities Playing surfaces should be dry, smooth and non-slip. Indoor surfaces should be dust-free.

Only approved stabilised posts should be used. Posts incorporating weights on the floor or on a base are dangerous.

Extra stabilising wires, linking posts to the floor or to the wall, should not be used.

Outdoor posts should be stabilised, but not with ropes or stakes.

Volleyball posts with winding handles must be folded correctly when not in use.

Equipment Trainer balls approved by the English Volleyball Association should be used for training and serving drills. Synthetic-leather and nylon balls cause bruising and discomfort.

Warm-up All players must do warm-up exercises before either practice or play. Volleyball is a strenuous game, and places considerable stress on ankles, knees and back.

Coaching Players should first be taught the basic skills of volleying, digging, serving, smashing and blocking, to ensure safe practice in a game.

When players are practising the smash or serve, they should be well spaced out and the ball should be aimed at an empty part of the court.

When players are practising the smash, the ball should never be returned to the server under the net, but by a round-the-court route. Accidents are frequently caused by players treading on the ball.

Players should never kick the ball.

Further information See **Further Reading**, page 107.

Weight Training

The term "weight training" covers any resistance-training exercise, including the use of barbells and dumb-bells (free weights) as well as fixed apparatus machines (multi-gyms). Very careful precautions are necessary to take account of each pupil's age, standard and level of physical development.

Weight training is safe if performed correctly. Teachers must understand the various techniques, together with the anatomical and physiological factors involved, and must be able to pass on this knowledge. They are strongly recommended to complete the teacher's award course of the British Amateur Weight Lifters' Association.

Equipment Metal parts must not be sharp. The ends of the bars should be rounded, and the discs should be checked for any roughness.

Collars should be checked for wear and damage to metal threads.

Machines should be regularly checked, including wires, cables, rotating sleeves and weight-stack pins.

Bars and barbells should be checked for weight, balance and the tightness of the collars before use. There must be sufficient spanners or keys for this purpose.

Machines using the weight-stack system must be checked to ensure that the inserted pins will not fall out. To help prevent such a problem, pupils should be taught to lower the weights with muscular control.

Hygiene should be a priority, particularly with benches and machines, where daily cleaning with disinfectant is recommended.

Storage Equipment should always be stored safely on a suitable rack, preferably in a lockable apparatus store.

Racks must be stable and strong enough to support a number of loaded bars. Unstored equipment should never be left unattended or in a position where it could be dangerous.

Care of the floor Free weights should always be placed on suitable mats (quilted agility mattresses are not suitable as their stitching can be damaged). Mats should be positioned so as to allow the lifter to stand on the floor while the weights are supported by mats.

Class organisation
- Pupils should only use weights under supervision, and should never handle them while they are in the apparatus store.
- One-handed barbell lifts should not be allowed in the early stages of weight training.
- Pupils should not attempt to lift a heavy weight before being thoroughly practised in a given technique.
- Lifters should keep at least two arms' lengths away from one another. Weight-stack machines should be well spaced.
- For all standing lifts, the lifter's feet should be on the floor and not on a mat.
- Spotters should be used when necessary, particularly on barbell lifts.

Weightlifting

Weightlifting includes the two Olympic lifts, together with strength tests and other competitive work with barbells and dumb-bells. The sport can be hazardous for adolescent pupils, where there is a particular danger of injuries to the spine. It must therefore be taught only by teachers who have been recognised by their school or LEA as being sufficiently experienced and knowledgeable. The minimum requirement for teaching weightlifting in schools is a teaching or coaching award from the British Amateur Weight Lifters' Association.

Overuse injury in young people is a very real problem. Overloading should be avoided, and competitive lifting should be delayed until skeletal growth is complete. Weightlifting competitions for young adults should not involve the lifting of more than the individual's own body weight. Any competition should preferably be judged on the style of lift rather than on the weight lifted.

Class organisation should be similar to that for weight training, but there is a greater need to work in groups with trained spotters. The emphasis in the early stages should be on skill and fitness.

Wrestling, Olympic-style

Olympic-style wrestling is the internationally agreed freestyle form of the sport used at the Olympic Games.

The rules are formulated so that two wrestlers can engage in hard physical combat without pain or injury. Submission, punching, kicking, high or heavy throws, or any move which will cause pain, are not allowed.

The Schoolboys' Olympic Wrestling Committee controls the sport for all boys of school age on behalf of the English Olympic Wrestling Association. It also organises instructor certificate courses for teachers.

Clothing Swimming trunks are ideal for training, and the wearing of shorts should be discouraged. Protective armpads or kneepads may be worn.

For competition there is a specially designed wrestling costume which is close-fitting and has short, tight-fitting legs. There should be no loose parts which can trap an opponent's fingers. A suitable support garment such as a jockstrap should always be worn.

A warm jersey or tracksuit is essential, especially for competitions.

Pupils should wear light shoes with smooth soles and without metal lace tags or eyelets. The basketball-type shoe with high sides is good, but pupils likely to enter competitions should wear specially designed wrestling boots with soft sides.

Facilities The wrestling area should measure at least 3 m x 3 m (10 ft x 10 ft). Mats should fulfil the requirements laid down by the British Amateur Wrestling Association, and should be suitable for use with wrestling boots.

Safe wrestling A wrestling class should never be left unattended or unsupervised.

Wrestlers in the under-17, under-15 and under-13 age groups are not allowed to execute any form of full-nelson or half-nelson which involves holding the chin with the other hand. Boys under 11 years of age are not allowed to use any form of nelson or bridging. Moves which put pressure on the neck or twist it are not allowed.

During training, teachers should watch out for any illegal or dangerous move.

Boys must be matched for a contest according to weight and age. Age groups are in two-year divisions, and weight groups are carefully arranged within these age divisions. In most competitions and championships an international pairing system is used which gives every boy at least two contests. No boy under 17 should normally be expected to take part in more than four contests in one day.

In a contest, supervision should be by a competent referee on the mat, and by a judge and a mat chairman at the edge of the mat. They should stop the match immediately if they think that any move or hold is causing pain or injury, or is likely to do so.

Part Five
Outdoor Pursuits

General

The growth in the range of outdoor pursuits, both within and outside the curriculum, has been one of the most significant developments in PE in recent years. Such pursuits now often form an integral part of environmental studies.

In any outdoor pursuit safety should be paramount, though not to the extent that this intimidates the beginner or destroys the spirit of adventure. Adequate preparation and safety measures will provide the basis for more ambitious work.

The growth of these activities in junior schools mirrors the same trend in the secondary sector, and has brought welcome curriculum innovation. Pursuits at junior level should involve less exposure to risk.

The basis of safety is good planning. When an accident is analysed, it usually turns out not to be a single isolated mishap, but rather the cumulative result of a succession of minor errors of judgement.

Experience is the greatest asset a leader can have in trying to anticipate events. Leaders should therefore have had considerable experience as assistant leaders before taking sole charge of a school group working in an unfamiliar area.

Everyone concerned with the administration and practice of outdoor pursuits should at least consult the following publications:

- the DES booklets *Learning Out-of-Doors* and *Safety in Outdoor Education* (see **Further Reading**, page 108);
- any equivalent document issued by the local LEA or EA;
- the literature issued by the appropriate national governing bodies.

Anyone in doubt should seek advice from the local LEA or EA Advisory service.

Teaching outdoor pursuits

Competence to lead Whenever possible, teachers should acquire the qualifications of the national governing body of the activity they are leading.

When headteachers are unsure about a teacher's competence to lead a particular outdoor activity, they should refer to the appropriate adviser, or failing that they should decide the matter on the basis of their personal knowledge of the teacher concerned. Their assessment should be guided by answers to the following questions:

- What relevant qualifications, skills and experience does the teacher have, including organisational skills?
- What knowledge or experience does the teacher have of the location that the party proposes to visit?
- What experience does the teacher have of working with pupils in the age-range of the party to be led?
- Does the teacher have a sense of responsibility and the right qualities for leadership?
- What is the teacher's present level of fitness?
- Does the teacher hold a first-aid qualification?

Administration and organisation Any teacher in an official school party has a duty of care (see page 13) with regard to the safety of the pupils concerned. This duty of care operates for 24 hours a day, every day, for the duration of the trip.

Teachers should ask senior colleagues for guidance, and should consider any general advice issued (or requirements laid down) by the LEA, EA, school board or governing body.

The following questions should be answered some weeks before departure:

- Has the trip been thoroughly organised and prepared, covering all details such as clothing, food and rest periods?
- Is the teacher–pupil ratio appropriate to the planned activity? The following factors must be considered here:
    — the nature of the activity
    — the degree of danger likely to be encountered
    — the experience and expertise of the staff involved
    — the ages and competence of the pupils.

As an illustration, 1:20 is a reasonable ratio for a party of 12-year-old pupils on a country walk in well-known, safe terrain, where no traffic or other foreseeable hazard is likely to be encountered. For slow learners or pupils with behavioural problems, a considerably reduced ratio might be needed, but this would depend on previous experience, the environment and the activity involved, and whether there is access to emergency assistance.

- Is there a schedule for continuous supervision?

- Will there be at least one teacher with each group who is trained in first aid, including resuscitation methods and treatment for exposure (see **First Aid**, page 30)?

- Have all emergency procedures been thoroughly considered, such as fire drill and accident drill? (Note that teachers may be injured as well as pupils.) And have suitable plans been prepared?

- Have potential weather conditions been taken into account? (This is particularly important in winter.)

- If the expedition is unaccompanied, are the safeguards adequate? Only when pupils have demonstrated sufficient skill, experience and maturity in a given activity while under supervision, should they be allowed to join an unaccompanied group. The number of pupils in the group will depend on the activity (see above).

- Is the insurance cover appropriate and adequate, including health cover and cover for teachers' own vehicles when conveying pupils (see page 30)?

- Have parents been informed, and have they signed the appropriate consent forms?

Parental consent

Page 86 gives two examples of the kind of document that might be sent to parents. Other examples of draft parental consent forms can be found in the DES booklet *Safety in Outdoor Education* (see **Further Reading**, page 108).

Trips overseas

When a party is travelling to another European Community country, the staff should be aware of the reciprocal health-insurance arrangements that apply (see DSS form E/111, available from post offices).

If a tour operator is being used, the firm should be a member of the Association of British Travel Agents (ABTA).

Because of various Home Office rulings, some pupils going on overseas trips may not qualify for inclusion on a collective United Kingdom passport. Unforeseen problems may arise for such children on seeking re-entry to the UK. In cases of doubt, enquiries should be made well in advance of the proposed trip to the Passport Office, Clive House, 70 Petty France, London SW1H 9HD.

Information to parents (example)

```
Dear Parent

It is hoped to include your child in the school party
proceeding to .................... on
................., and he or she may have the
opportunity to participate in the following activities:

1 ..............................
2 ..............................
3 ..............................
4 ..............................

There will be .......... boys and .......... girls in
the party, together with .......... members of staff.
The teacher in charge will be .........................

In your child's interests, it is important that you
should sign the attached agreement form and declare any
known medical condition from which your child may be
suffering, with an indication of any medication which
he or she may be receiving.

Yours sincerely

Headteacher
```

Parental consent form (example)

My son/daughter is in good health and I consider him/her capable of taking part in the activities as detailed in your letter dated ....

In the event of illness or an accident, I consent to any necessary medical treatment, which might include the use of anaesthetics.

I agree to my son/daughter taking part in the school activity as detailed in your letter dated ....

Signed .... Parent/Guardian

Address and Telephone number
....
....
....

Please complete and return this form to the headteacher, together with any relevant information concerning your child's health.

Please declare any known medical condition and any medication which he or she is receiving.

Camping

Camping takes many different forms, and can involve a variety of hazards. Some dangers arise directly from camping activities such as cooking or the management of fires and stoves; others are linked to associated activities such as bathing and climbing.

Group leaders should consult the Duke of Edinburgh's Award *Expedition Guide* (see **Further Reading**, page 108). For camping in wild terrain, leaders should also consult the *Mountain Walking Leader Training Scheme* (see **Further Reading**, page 108).

Competence to lead The party leader should be experienced in all aspects of camping, and should have made a prior visit to (or have prior knowledge of) the site to be used. For camping in mountainous country, leaders should be appropriately trained and experienced, and should hold a mountain leadership logbook (see **Climbing and Mountain-walking**, page 94). If the group is camping near water and pursues water-borne activities, the leader must have knowledge of safe practice in those pursuits.

Staff–pupil ratio A ratio of one teacher to ten pupils is recommended, but this depends on local conditions, and on the age and ability of the pupils. Mixed parties should be accompanied by staff of both sexes. Ideally there should be at least two responsible adults in case one of them suffers illness or accident.

Planning Adequate planning, training and preparation is essential. In particular, there should be a practice drill in the use of cooking stoves, in the pitching and striking of tents, and in the packing of loads.

The leader must ensure that the equipment and clothing are suitable for the type of camp.

The equipment should be tested and checked before departure.

On site The leader should ensure the following:

- A first camp should be held under controlled conditions, and should be located near to permanent shelter.
- Tents should be pitched sufficiently far apart to prevent the spread of fire and to allow free movement.
- Instructions should be given on hygiene to cover all aspects of sewage and rubbish disposal, waste pits, personal appearance and the general appearance of the camp.
- Ball games and running should be banned in the vicinity of tents.

- No cooking should be allowed inside the tents unless absolutely necessary, and only then if prior training has been given.
- Petrol stoves have led to serious problems in the past, and are not recommended for a youth group.
- Gas cylinders and fuel for stoves should be stored outside the tents, and containers should be clearly marked — for example, "methylated spirits" or "paraffin".
- Permission should be obtained from the owner of any site before open fires are lit, and care should be taken to prevent any fire from spreading.
- No form of lighting that involves a naked flame should be permitted inside the tents.
- The leader should know the location and phone number of the nearest doctor and hospital.

Further reading See **Further Reading**, page 108.

Canoeing

Canoeing, like any other water-borne activity, involves a definite element of risk, and must therefore be properly organised. Reasonable precautions must be taken without detracting from the spirit of adventure that is associated with the handling of small craft. Common sense and consideration for others are needed at all times.

Competence to lead For general leadership in outdoor pursuits, see page 84. In addition, the British Canoe Union recommends the following qualifications:

- For open-cockpit kayaks or canoes on placid water:
    - placid-water teacher.
- For closed- or open-cockpit kayaks or canoes on very sheltered water:
    - canoeing supervisor
    - trainee instructor/trainee senior instructor.
- For grade-one water or sheltered coastal areas:
    - instructor.
- For proficiency-level expeditions, surfing and open-water canoeing:
    - senior instructor.
- For touring marathon and sprint-racing activities:
    - placid-water senior instructor.

All leaders must be able to perform expired-air resuscitation, and must know how to recognise and treat hypothermia.

Staff–pupil ratio A ratio of one leader to eight pupils is recommended on still waters, and one to six on running or tidal waters. On exposed water an assistant leader with the ability to perform deep-water rescues would be appropriate.

Clothing and equipment A waterproof anorak is essential. This should not hamper movement, but should ensure warmth and protection from the elements. UK waters are always cold, and special consideration is needed to ensure adequate warm clothing for extended periods afloat.

Crash helmets are essential for paddling on white water, and are strongly recommended for surfing. Gum boots or heavy clothing must never be worn. Lightweight footwear is essential.

Canoeists must always wear a lifejacket or personal buoyancy aid that conforms either to the standard BCU/BCMA BA83 or to British Standard 3595. The latter is advised for sea expeditions.

On every expedition the leader must carry:

- a first-aid kit
- a tow line
- distress flares for sea and open water
- spare paddles and spray cover
- an exposure bag
- equipment for making hot drinks.

On extended expeditions every person in the group should carry all these items. The leader of each group (see page 90) must also carry a whistle.

The canoe

Buoyancy All canoes should be fitted with buoyancy equipment. If buoyancy bags are used, they should be firmly secured and distributed properly between bow and stern, with 13.5 kg (30 lb) at either end, so that in the event of a capsize they:

- remain in place
- do not suffer damage as a result of water pressure
- cause the canoe to float horizontally.

Toggles and painters If the kayaks carry a fore and aft painter, these must be secured to keep them well clear of the cockpit. Toggles are preferable.

Spray covers The use of spray covers for the cockpit is strongly recommended, and these must be used if waves are likely to be encountered. Covers should be easily removable. They may not be appropriate for first-time canoeists.

Waterproof bags/containers All items which may be damaged by getting wet should be packed in waterproof bags or containers. Equipment must be stored in such a way that the kayak is kept in trim, and must be secured so that it stays firmly in place in the event of a capsize. Equipment must not be packed in the cockpit of a kayak or beside the paddler's legs.

Footrests These should be very substantial, and should be designed to prevent the canoeist sliding forward on impact. They should be easily adjustable, and should not be able to rotate.

Colour A canoe or kayak must be brightly coloured.

Glass-reinforced plastic (GRP) construction Builders of glass-reinforced plastic craft such as canoes or dinghies should be aware of the hazards involved, such as dangerous catalysts, skin irritations from chemicals and dust, and the fire risk associated with resins. BS 4163 (1975) refers to these hazards. The Health and Safety Executive and the local fire officer should be consulted before fibreglass or resins are used for repairs or construction work.

Capsize drill Capsize drill must form an early part of basic training, and must be practised thoroughly.

In the event of a capsize, the kayak should be left upside-down for use as a buoyancy aid, and the canoeist should stay with the boat. Only in exceptional circumstances should this rule be waived, such as when the kayak is drifting towards a dangerous obstacle such as a sluice or weir.

If the capsize happens close to land, the canoeist should move to one end, lightly hold the kayak, and tow it to shore while swimming using a back stroke.

For trips on open water, the group must have mastered deep-water rescue methods.

Before setting out The leader must do the following:

- Check the condition and suitability of canoes, equipment and clothing (windproof anorak, wetsuit, footwear etc).

- Decide whether members of the party have sufficient experience to go out in the prevailing weather and water conditions.

- Find out about local conditions, including currents, tides and dangerous features such as weirs, by studying maps, guides, charts and tide tables.

- Obtain local weather forecasts, available in coastal areas from Marine Call (see the appropriate local telephone directory).

- Arrange a signalling system within the group.

- Give details to the local coastguard or police of any route to be followed on unsheltered waters (eg a coastal trip), or of any passage across a large area of exposed inland water. The same authorities must also be informed of the party's safe return.

On the water The leader should ensure the following:

- Good discipline must be maintained throughout.

- Large parties should be split into groups of six to eight under competent leaders.

- The slowest paddlers should go at the front of each group, and the slower groups should go first.

- Each group should keep together in a predetermined formation.

- The leader of each group should be positioned according to the wind and current, and to the configuration of the group.

- A leading canoeist and a last canoeist should be appointed from among responsible members in each group, with the task of ensuring that the group stays together.

- At the top of rapids an inspection should be carried out, from the bank if necessary. The canoeists should then descend singly, and wait in the slack water below until the whole party is safely through.

- Stops should be made in sheltered places, and extra clothing should be put on when necessary.

- Mishaps should be dealt with quickly to prevent the remainder of the party getting cold.

Further reading See **Further Reading**, page 108.

Caving and Potholing

Competence to lead For general leadership in outdoor pursuits, see page 84.

The recommended qualification, awarded by the National Caving Association, is the Cave Instructor's Certificate. An assistant instructor must at the very least be able in an emergency to bring the party back to the surface safely without the leader, and must have a thorough knowledge of the relevant cave-rescue procedures.

Staff–pupil ratio The minimum safe ratio in easy cave systems is two competent adults to ten pupils. This applies to systems in which the party would be able to get out safely at any stage without the adults. Group numbers must be reduced if the cave system demands it. The party must consist of a minimum of four people.

Safety Underground systems present not only most of the hazards associated with mountains, but also those associated with water, together with one or two other dangers. Rescue can sometimes be near-impossible, even from places which can normally be reached easily by a fit party. Leaders must always bear this in mind when planning their trips. Caving can rarely be absolutely safe, but leaders should ensure that the risks are acceptable.

Equipment The minimum equipment for each individual is:

- warm clothing and a protective overgarment
- a protective helmet with a chinstrap and lamp bracket
- boots, preferably with commando-type soles
- an efficient headlamp, preferably electric.

If there is any possibility of prolonged exposure to water, then a wetsuit, exposure suit or other suitable gear must be worn.

Each member of the party must carry lighting spares, a whistle and emergency food. Rope, ladders and other equipment should be taken as required. The leader must also carry a first-aid kit.

Novice parties No leader should take a novice party into any system with which he or she is unfamiliar, or which the party would find difficult.

Novices on their first trip should be monitored for signs of physical weakness, reckless behaviour, claustrophobia, poor reaction to wet or cold, or any other symptoms likely to hinder their progress on subsequent trips.

Before going underground The leader should:

- Check that the cave owner has given permission to descend.
- Brief the party on all the relevant safety and cave-conservation precautions, giving details of the route to be followed and the features which will be encountered.

- Check the equipment and clothing of all members of the party, ensuring that their helmets fit correctly and their lights are working.

- Check carefully, both from weather forecasts and from direct observation, that there is no chance of the system becoming flooded.

- Leave a note with a responsible adult giving the passages to be followed, the expected time of return, the number in the party, the group's level of experience and the equipment being taken.

- Leave an identifying object (or person) at the entrance of any cave that is entered.

While underground The leader must:

- Maintain constant contact with the front and rear of the party.

- Monitor the morale and condition of the party, and be prepared to turn back at any stage.

- Make the party fully aware of any dangers of loose chokes, falling rocks (especially below pitches), static or flowing sumps, or false flooring.

- Take special care to avoid even minor injuries which could require a major rescue.

- Protect all places where a slip could lead to injury, using a lifeline, a hand-line or some other method.

- Report back to those concerned when the party returns.

Vertical pitches
- Ladder pitches or roped climbing should first be taught and practised above ground in caving gear.

- The time required for each ladder pitch should be estimated in advance, and the trip and the group size planned accordingly. Long waits underground should be avoided, particularly if the participants are wet.

- All ladder pitches must be lifelined using the accepted safe techniques. Lifelines should be held by experienced cavers or by competent pupils under constant supervision. No one should be allowed on wire ladders in hook-lacing boots.

- An experienced caver must descend first and ascend last, and a second experienced caver should descend last and ascend first.

Mines Mines often present totally different dangers and problems from those encountered in natural systems, and must be treated with the greatest respect. Coal mines should never be used for caving. Advice should be sought from the local Inspectorate of Mines and Quarries, which can be found in the local telephone directory under Health and Safety Executive.

94 *Part Five:* Outdoor Pursuits

Further reading See **Further Reading**, page 108.

Climbing and Mountain-walking

Competence to lead For general leadership in outdoor pursuits see page 84.

The Mountain Walking Leader Training Board issues a logbook to anyone who pursues a leadership course which it has approved. This will indicate the suitability of the person to lead. Full information is available from the Board itself. The Mountain Walking Leader Training Awards form a national yardstick against which standards are measured.

All teachers who accompany climbing or mountain-walking groups on the fells or mountains should be trained in first aid, including the treatment for hypothermia.

Staff–pupil ratios

Field trips In less mountainous areas with easy access to main roads, and given reasonable weather conditions, a staff–pupil ratio of 1:15 is realistic for most types of fieldwork, but with a minimum of *two* adults. (The party should also be suitably dressed and shod.)

In more demanding terrain, the recommended ratio is ten pupils to one competent member of staff.

Fell-walking (hill-walking) The number of young people to one leader should never be more than ten. In unaccompanied expedition groups, the group should number no fewer than four and no more than seven.

Rock-climbing See opposite.

Clothing and equipment Waterproof and windproof clothing and a spare jersey are needed, even in summer. Boots with vibram-type soles are essential. Crampons and an ice-axe are required for snow and ice.

Each member of the group should carry the following:

- a map and compass
- a whistle
- a pencil and paper
- suitable food and drink
- a torch (this must be in working order, and must have been safeguarded against being accidentally switched on in the rucksack).

Every group should carry the following between them:

- first-aid equipment
- a polythene survival bag measuring 2.5 m x 1.2 m (8 ft x 4 ft) x 800 gauge for every two members of the group
- extra food and items such as glucose tablets or sweets.

In winter conditions sleeping bags should be carried. In areas where difficult scrambling terrain may be encountered, 35 m (38 yd) of 9-mm or No 3 climbing rope is desirable.

For climbing equipment, see below.

Before setting out
- The leader should check local weather forecasts and conditions, and the location of all local mountain-rescue posts.
- Whenever possible, information should be left at base camp, including a route card indicating where the group is going and when it is expected to return. If plans are changed, word should be sent back. The route card should be collected on return to base.

On the fells (hills)
- During the walk, the pace should be reasonable for the slowest member of the party. No one should become detached from the group, and everyone should be aware of the procedure to be followed in case of accident.
- If any member of the group shows signs of exhaustion, particularly in worsening weather, the party should seek some shelter from the wind and wait for an improvement in conditions.

Rock-climbing

Tuition Rock-climbing must only be taught by suitably experienced instructors. The British Mountaineering Council (BMC) provides rock-climbing awards, and there are a number of local training schemes.

Supervision On one-pitch climbs, such as low crags, artificial climbing walls or climbing towers, one leader should be responsible for no more than four pupils.

On longer climbs, one leader should be responsible for no more than three pupils, and each climber should be belayed individually. Climbers must remain roped throughout the climb.

When major crags are attempted, there must be at least two adult leaders in the party.

Equipment Only approved equipment should be used, all of which must be checked by the leader. It must include BSI-specification safety helmets for all climbers, gloves for belaying, and waist-harnesses with a screw-gate karabiner. Footwear should provide good ankle support and good adhesion or grip on the rock.

For climbing and abseiling, No 4 or 11-mm hawser-laid or kernmantel climbing ropes must be used, together with screw-gate karabiners approved by the UIAA (*Union Internationale des Associations d'Alpinisme*, or International Union of Mountaineering Associations).

Ropes should not be allowed to run through a loop of nylon or perlon. A screw-gate karabiner should be interposed between the running rope and the loop.

Ropes must be inspected at regular intervals for wear and tear, and records of rope usage must be entered in a log.

On the rock-face The leader must ensure the following:

- The grade of the climb must be within the capability of the least-able climber in the group.
- Climbing or "bouldering" must never take place unless the leader is present.
- No one should lead a climb without the leader's permission.
- All knots should be checked by the leader before and during the climb.
- The standard climbing call system within the party should be observed.
- Abseiling must always be supervised by the leaders. A safety rope must be used for abseiling, and must be belayed separately from the abseil rope.

Rock-climbing walls Rock-climbing walls should only be used under the supervison of leaders with the appropriate qualifications or experience. Ropes and equipment should be of the same standard as that required for rock-climbing.

The climbing wall should be approved by the LEA or the BMC, and should be regularly inspected and maintained.

Further reading See **Further Reading**, pages 108–9.

Orienteering

Competence to lead For general leadership in outdoor pursuits see page 84.

The recommended qualification awarded by the British Orienteering Federation (BOF) is the British Orienteering Instructors' Certificate. However, evidence of experience and competence is adequate for teaching a basic introduction to the sport.

Clothing Footwear should be suitable for the course terrain and the prevailing weather conditions.

Adequate clothing should be worn to suit the prevailing weather conditions. Complete arm and leg cover is recommended for most forest events.

In competition, all participants should carry a whistle.

Course planning and preparation The organiser should ensure the following:

- Prior permission should always have been obtained to use a given course, either from the landowners or from the managing agents concerned. The existence of orienteering maps does not necessarily indicate any right of access. Permission for access must be sought on every occasion.

- Local advice must be sought and taken.

- Competitors must not be asked to cross busy roads or negotiate major geographical hazards. Any hazards should be marked on competitors' maps, and should be brought to their notice in the pre-start area.

- Courses should be appropriate to the age and experience of those taking part. Control points should be located well away from deep water, unsafe buildings or concealed drops in ground level.

- Only experienced participants should take part in night-time orienteering. They should compete in pairs or in groups, and should keep together.

- The address and telephone number of the nearest doctor should be displayed at base, together with the location of the nearest telephone.

- The organiser should have access to a first-aid box.

- If a participant fails to check in by close-out time, sufficient competent personnel must be prepared to search the area under the direction of the organiser.

Sailing

These notes apply to dinghy sailing and windsurfing only.

Competence to lead For general leadership in outdoor pursuits see page 84.

The recommended qualifications of the Royal Yachting Association (RYA) and the National Schools Sailing Association (NSSA) are:

- for sailing inland:
    — Senior Instructor/Sailing Master;
- for tidal sailing:
    — Senior Instructor/Sailing Master endorsed for tidal waters;
- for windsurfing (RYA):
    — Sailboard Instructor.

Clothing Clothing should be warm, and should be protected by waterproofs when necessary. At certain times of the year in some areas, wetsuits may be essential.

Personal buoyancy Whatever the weather conditions, instructors and crews should wear a personal buoyancy aid that conforms to either BS 3595 (1981 or later) or SBBNF (1979 or later). All crew must be competent, must be confident in the water, and should have practised swimming with a personal buoyancy aid before taking part in sailing or windsurfing.

Boat safety The instructor must ensure that all craft are seaworthy, with adequate and secure buoyancy-aid equipment to meet emergencies.

The recommended number of crew per boat during instruction is detailed in the booklet on the RYA/NSSA National Proficiency Scheme (see **Further Reading**, page 109).

Capsize Capsize procedure should be explained in the training programme, and should then be practised. In the event of a capsize, all crew must stay with the boat.

Before launch Instructors should take local knowledge into account, and should always read or listen to local weather reports (available in coastal areas from Marine Call; see the appropriate local telephone directory).

Whenever a group sails in open coastal or tidal waters, the leader should submit complete details of the fleet and of the itinerary to the coastguard before sailing; all craft must keep to an agreed formation.

On the water There should be a well-defined sailing area, which should be known to all concerned and strictly observed.

A simple code of easily visible and/or audible signals should be understood and used by all crew.

In offshore winds, special attention must be given to group control.

Safety boats The presence of an appropriately equipped and manned safety boat is essential. Advice on the type of craft needed is given in the NSSA booklet *Safety Afloat* (see **Further Reading**, page 109). The RYA Rescue Boat Coxswain's Award is a useful qualification.

First aid All sailing instructors should have expertise in first aid (see page 30), and especially in the following:

- applying expired-air resuscitation
- stopping severe bleeding
- recognising hypothermia at an early stage, and taking preventive measures
- treating shock
- applying inflatable splints in the case of a fracture.

Further reading See **Further Reading**, page 109.

Skiing

Competence to lead For general leadership in outdoor pursuits see page 84.

For organisers of ski courses abroad, the English Ski Council (ESC) recommends the Ski Course Organiser's Certificate (Part 1) as an appropriate qualification.

For organisers of ski courses on recognised pistes in Scotland, the appropriate qualification is the Ski Leader's Award of the Scottish National Ski Council (SNSC).

All leaders should have read the *Ski Course Organisers' Handbook* (see **Further Reading**, page 109).

For the teaching of skiing on artificial ski slopes, the Artificial Ski Slope Instructor's Award organised by the ESC is recommended.

Instructors who teach skiing on snow should hold at least the BASI III Award of the British Association of Ski Instructors (BASI).

If a teacher is required to supervise any practice sessions that may be arranged to follow the formal instruction by a qualified ski instructor, then that teacher should have attended an LEA or EA Ski-course Organiser's Course (Part 1).

Clothing Ski clothing must offer adequate protection against snow, wind and cold. A distinctive garment such as a red bobble-hat will help identification. Gloves are essential; ski goggles and sun cream are recommended, and are essential later in the season as the sun becomes stronger.

Equipment
- The boots must give firm support to the ankles and lower legs, and must be compatible with the bindings.
- The skis must never be longer than the height of the skier.
- The release bindings must be properly adjusted so that the release mechanisms work correctly.
- For safety, retaining straps or ski brakes must always be fitted to the skis.
- The length of ski sticks should be roughly equivalent to waist height.

Physical preparation All skiing trips should be preceded by a programme of regular pre-ski exercises and fitness-training sessions. Work on artificial ski slopes will provide valuable experience; a ratio of one instructor to twelve pupils is recommended on such slopes.

Skiing on snow

In Britain A day's skiing on local fells should be planned in the same way as a day's mountaineering. Pupils should be properly clothed against bad weather, and should take sufficient food, hot drinks and spare clothing with them.

The party should be self-supporting. Party leaders should carry emergency equipment as for mountain work (shelter, spare clothing, food, first aid and communication equipment), and should know how to move an injured person.

The group should be adequately supervised, and should stay together.

Skiing abroad The following details should be checked at the planning stage:
- the proximity of the hotel or chalet accommodation to the ski slopes, and the associated lift facilities;
- the availability of adequate drying and storage facilities for clothes, boots and skis;
- fire safety in the hotel or chalet accommodation;
- adequate insurance cover;

- the reliability of the ski-tour operator — is it, for example, a member of the Association of British Travel Agents (ABTA), or is it included in the list of approved operators compiled by the LEA and/or the School and Group Travel Association (SAGTA)?

Safety on the slopes
- Ski slopes are operated according to internationally recognised safety rules, which all group members must know.
- All pupils must know the Skiway Code, which is available on video from the ESC.
- All skiing must be graded according to the standard of the pupil.
- Tired skiers should never be allowed to continue skiing.

Tuition Tuition must be by qualified instructors. Four hours' tuition (two hours in the morning and two in the afternoon) is often provided. If only two hours' tuition is given and the pupils are allowed on the slopes at other times, then they must be supervised by teachers who have adequate experience and knowledge of the area, and who meet the requirements laid down above (see **Competence to lead**, page 99).

Off-the-slope supervision Adequate supervision in the hotel and resort must be maintained at all times, including during any evening entertainment or activity.

Emergency and accident procedures The party should include a member of staff who knows first aid and can treat minor ailments. A range of appropriate medicines should be included.

All members of the party should be familiar with accident and emergency procedures for personal accident and fire.

Fire drill should be practised within 24 hours of arrival at the resort.

Further reading See **Further Reading**, page 109.

Sub-aqua Diving and Snorkelling

Competence to lead For general leadership in outdoor pursuits see page 84.

The British Sub Aqua Club (BSAC) recommends the following qualifications:

Pupil Grade	Instructor Grade
Snorkeller Award	Snorkel Instructor Certificate
Advanced Snorkeller Award	Advanced Snorkel Instructor Certificate
Aqualung Training in the Pool	BSAC Club Instructor
Open-water Diving	BSAC Advanced Instructor

Pupils	All snorkellers must be able to swim 50 m (55 yd).

All scuba divers should be over 15 years of age, and should have taken the British sub-aqua proficiency test.

Pupils with epilepsy, diabetes or certain other conditions must not be allowed to take part.

All divers should know the techniques of rescue and expired-air resuscitation. |
| **Staff–pupil ratio** | The recommended ratios are: |
| *Pool training* | Snorkelling: one instructor for up to ten pupils.

Aqualung training: one instructor for up to four pupils. |
| *Open-water diving and training* | Snorkelling: one instructor for up to four pupils.

Aqualung diving: one instructor for no more than two pupils. |
| **Clothing and equipment** | When diving takes place in UK waters, some form of protective clothing such as a drysuit or wetsuit should be worn.

All equipment, including masks, snorkels and aqualungs, should conform to the appropriate BSI specifications.

All divers should wear suitable lifejackets (CO_2- or air-inflated), and each aqualung group should use a surface marker buoy. |
| **Emergencies** | Before any training or diving can take place, whether in the pool or in open water, it is essential to make adequate emergency provisions, including training in the appropriate safety drills. |
| **Open-water dives** | A support boat should always be present, with at least one stand-by diver.

The leader or instructor should be satisfied that the pupils are physically fit enough to take part in a particular dive. No one should be allowed to dive who is suffering from fatigue, or from a cold or other infection.

Divers should normally work in pairs, whether for snorkelling or for aqualung diving. Diving without a partner should only be allowed when a lifeline is used and an experienced standby diver is available.

All divers should observe the British Sub Aqua Club Code of Conduct, which is contained in the *Diving Instructor's Manual* (see **Further Reading**, page 109). |

The skipper of the boat used by the divers should be suitably qualified and experienced. BSAC Diver Coxswain Level III is recommended.

Outdoor Pursuits Not Included in This Book

When any activity is planned that has not been dealt with in this book, reference should be made to the general sections on pages 83–6, paying particular attention to the matter of teacher–pupil ratios.

Leaders should take note of any recommendations issued by the governing body of the sport in question, and should also refer to the DES booklet *Safety in Outdoor Education*. For aspects of outdoor education not covered here, it may be helpful to consult the Duke of Edinburgh's Award Scheme booklet *Outdoor Education Safety and Good Practice*. For further details of these and other publications, see **Further Reading**, page 108.

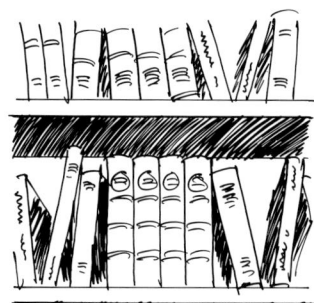

Further Reading

Part One — PE, the Law and Safe Practice

PE and the law
Your Legal Position in Teaching, John Hodgson & John Tingle (New Education Press, 1989).

Headteacher's Legal Guide, National Association of Head Teachers (Croner Publications, 1984).

Teachers and the Law, G. R. Barrell (Methuen, 1985).

Health and Safety at Work etc Act 1974 (HMSO).

PE for pupils with SEN
Physical Education for Children with Special Educational Needs in Mainstream Education (BAALPE, 1989).

British Journal of Physical Education — Supplement on Special Needs (Physical Education Association of Great Britain and Northern Ireland).

Profiles of Functional Ability (British Sports Association for the Disabled).

BSAD Rules and Procedures Handbook (British Sports Association for the Disabled, 1990).

Swimming and Epilepsy (Sports Council/British Epilepsy Association, 1987).

Health Education Project Newsletter Nos 24 & 25 (Health Education Authority/Physical Education Association of Great Britain and Northern Ireland, March & May 1990).

First aid
Sport First Aid Parts 1 & 2, Xavier Flanagan (Dublin University).

Safety and Injury (National Coaching Foundation: Introductory Study Pack 3, 1984).

Essentials of First Aid, C. C. Molloy (St John Ambulance, 1987).

First Aid Manual: Emergency Procedures for Everyone at Home, at Work or at Leisure, St John Ambulance/St Andrew's Ambulance Association/British Red Cross Society (Dorling Kindersley, 1987).

Part Three — Swimming and Diving

ASA Handbook (Amateur Swimming Association).

Safety in Swimming Pools (Sports Council/HSE, 1988).

Swimming and Epilepsy (Sports Council/British Epilepsy Association, 1987).

Pool Lifeguarding (Royal Lifesaving Society, 1989).

A Guide to the Safety Signs Regulations (HSE, 1980).

Part Four — Games and Sports

Conduct and supervision
Safety in Physical Education, DES (HMSO, 1973).

Working with Children (National Coaching Foundation: Introductory Study Pack 7, 1989).

Numerous leaflets produced by the National Playing Fields Association.

Archery
Archery Today (Grand National Archery Society, 1988).

Athletics
Athletics — Keep It Safe, David Couling & Douglas Dickenson (Amateur Athletic Association, 1990).

AAA Rules for Competition, in *AAA/WAAA Handbook* (Amateur Athletic Association).

Facilities for Athletics — Track and Field, R. B. Gooch (Amateur Athletic Association/National Playing Fields Association, 1986).

Basketball
Basketball Curriculum Guide, ed. Brian Coleman (English Basketball Association, 1989).

Cycling
Cycle Safety leaflets (Royal Society for the Prevention of Accidents).

Advice sheets on the organisation of cyclo-cross, time trials, circuit and track racing (English Schools Cycling Association).

Information leaflets from the British Cycling Federation.

Cycling Teaching Certificate Syllabus.

Martial arts
Skilful Karate, Greg McLatchie (A & C Black, out of print).

Guidelines for Safety Within the Martial Arts (Martial Arts Commission, 1990).

Netball
Netball Rules for Young Players (English Schools Netball Association/All England Netball Association, 1985).

The Netball Coaching Manual, All England Netball Association (A & C Black, 1984).

GCSE Curriculum Guide to Netball (All England Netball Association, in preparation 1990).

Rowing
Code of Practice for Water Safety (Amateur Rowing Association).

Rugby Union and Rugby League
Player Improvement Plan 1989/90 (Rugby Football Union).

Positional Skills, ed. Neil Pidduck (Rugby Football Union, 1980).

Rugby League (A & C Black: *Know the Game* series, out of print).

Injury Prevention leaflets (Rugby Football Union).

Volleyball
GCSE Volleyball, ed. David Joy (English Volleyball Association, 1988).

Part Five — Outdoor Pursuits

General
Learning Out-of-Doors: Survey of Outdoor Education and Short Stay Residential Experiences, DES (HMSO, 1985).

Safety in Outdoor Education, DES (HMSO, 1989).

Outdoor Education Safety and Good Practice (Duke of Edinburgh's Award Scheme, 1988).

Out and About, M. O'Conner, (Methuen, 1987).

Safe Principles in Outdoor Education (National Association of Outdoor Education, 1988).

Camping
Expedition Guide, Wally Keay (Duke of Edinburgh's Award Scheme, 1987).

Camping and Education, Ministry of Education (HMSO, 1961, out of print).

Canoeing
Canoeing Handbook, compiled by Ray Rowe (British Canoe Union, 1990).

The Water Sports Code (Central Council for Physical Recreation, out of print).

Caving and potholing
Cave Instructor's Certificate Scheme Handbook (National Caving Association).

Local Cave Leader's Assessment Scheme Handbook (National Caving Association).

First Annual Report of the National Caving Association Radon Working Party (National Caving Association, 1990).

Climbing and mountain-walking
Mountaincraft and Leadership Handbook, E. Langmuir (Mountain Walking Leader Training Board/Scottish Sports Council, 1984).

Mountain Walking Leader Training Scheme (Mountain Walking Leader Training Board, 1990).

Safety on Mountains, J. Jackson, rev. T. Jepson (British Mountaineering Council, 1989).

Sailing
Safety Afloat (National Schools Sailing Association).

RYA/NSSA National Proficiency Scheme Handbook (Royal Yachting Association/National Schools Sailing Association).

The Water Sports Code (Central Council for Physical Recreation, out of print).

Windsurfing Safety Guide (Department of Transport [HM Coastguard], 1990).

Small Craft Safety Checklist (Department of Transport [HM Coastguard], 1990).

Yacht and Boat Safety Scheme (Department of Transport [HM Coastguard], 1990).

Skiing
Ski Course Organisers' Handbook (English Ski Council, 1989).

Skiway Code (video) (English Ski Council).

Sub-aqua Diving and Snorkelling
Diving Instructor's Manual, J. Hazzard (British Sub Aqua Club, 1983).

Useful Addresses

British Association of Advisers
and Lecturers in Physical
Education
Nelson House
6 The Beacon
Exmouth
Devon
EX8 2AG

Central Council for Physical
Recreation[1]
Francis House
Francis Street
London
SW1 1DE

Department of Education and
Science
Elizabeth House
York Road
London
SE1 7PH

Scottish Education Department
New St Andrew's House
St James Centre
Edinburgh
EH1 3SY

Education Department
Welsh Office
Phase 2
Government Buildings
Ty Glas Road
Llanishen
Cardiff
CF4 5WE

Department of Education
Northern Ireland
Rathgall House
Ballow Road
Bangor
Co Down
BT19 2PR

Physical Education
Association of Great Britain
and Northern Ireland
162 Kings Cross Road
London
WC1X 9DH

The Sports Council
16 Upper Woburn Place
London
WC1H 0QP

---

[1] The addresses of national governing bodies of sport and other relevant organisations can be obtained from the CCPR.

Useful Addresses

Scottish Sports Council
Caledonia House
South Gyle
Edinburgh
EH12 9DQ

Sports Council for Wales
National Sports Centre for Wales
Sophia Gardens
Cardiff
CF1 9SW

Sports Council for Northern Ireland
House of Sport
Upper Malone Road
Belfast
BT9 5LA

Royal Society for the Prevention of Accidents
Cannon House
The Priory
Queensway
Birmingham
B4 6PS

The Duke of Edinburgh's Award Scheme
5 Prince of Wales Terrace
Kensington
London
W8 5PG

The National Coaching Foundation
4 College Close
Beckett Park
Leeds
LS6 3QH

Gaelic Athletic Association (Northern Ireland)
c/o Sports Council for Northern Ireland
House of Sport
Upper Malone Road
Belfast
BT9 5LA

School and Group Travel Association Ltd
Honeycroft House
Pangbourne Road
Upper Basildon
Nr Pangbourne
Berkshire
RG8 8LR